Tchaikovsky

HIS LIFE & MUSIC

Jeremy Siepmann

Author's Acknowledgments

All books are a team effort. This one would not have been possible without the tireless support of my editors Genevieve Helsby and Anthony Short, and my wife Deborah, all of whose combination of unwavering standards, imaginative suggestions and inspiring erudition has been both a pleasure and a privilege from the outset. And last, but very far from least, I am indebted to Klaus Heymann, founder and CEO of Naxos Records, who came up with the idea in the first place.

If the CD included with this book is missing, broken, or defective, please email customer.service@sourcebooks.com for a replacement. Please include your name and address, and the ISBN number located on the back cover of this book.

Published by Sourcebooks MediaFusion, an imprint of Sourcebooks, Inc.
P.O. Box 4410, Naperville, Illinois 60567-4410
(630) 961-3900
Fax: (630) 961-2168
www.sourcebooks.com

Originally published in the UK by Naxos Books.

Library of Congress Cataloging-in-Publication Data

Siepmann, Jeremy.
Tchaikovsky : his life and music / by Jeremy Siepmann.
p. cm.
Includes bibliographical references (p.) and index.
ISBN 978-1-4022-1001-3 (hardcover : alk. paper) 1. Tchaikovsky, Peter Ilich, 1840-1893. 2. Composers--Russia--Biography. I. Title.

ML410.C4S52 2007
780.92--dc22
[B]

2007025791

Printed and bound in the United States of America.
LT 10 9 8 7 6 5 4 3 2 1

Contents

i Website
ii On CD One
iv On CD Two
vi Preface

1 **Chapter 1:** Childhood, Boyhood, Youth 1840–1864
22 Interlude I: Tchaikovsky at the Piano
29 **Chapter 2:** Coming of Age 1865–1876
49 Interlude II: Tchaikovsky in the Theatre
57 **Chapter 3:** Celebrity and Crisis 1876–1877
76 Interlude III: Tchaikovsky and the Orchestra
87 **Chapter 4:** Sex, Suffering, Sublimation and Loss 1878–1884
103 Interlude IV: The Chamber Music
107 **Chapter 5:** House, Home and Happiness 1885–1888
124 Interlude V: Tchaikovsky in Song
133 **Chapter 6:** The New Statesman: At Home and Abroad 1888–1891
152 Interlude VI: Tchaikovsky and Russianness
159 **Chapter 7:** Morbidity, Mortality and Myth 1891–1893
178 **Epilogue:** Tchaikovsky and Posterity

183 The Western Background
195 The Russian Cultural Background
201 Personalities
209 Selected Bibliography
210 Glossary
216 Annotations of CD Tracks
229 Index

www.naxos.com/naxosbooks/tchaikovskylifeandmusic

Visit the dedicated website for *Tchaikovsky: His Life and Music* and gain free access to the following:

- **Hours more music to listen to – historical and modern recordings**
- **Music by some of Tchaikovsky's contemporaries**
- **A timeline of Tchaikovsky's life, set alongside contemporary events in arts, culture and politics**

To access this you will need:

- **ISBN: 97818437921195**
- **Password: Nutcracker**

www.naxos.com/naxosbooks/tchaikovskylifeandmusic

On CD One

1	**Zemfira's Song** Ljuba Kazarnovskaya, soprano; Ljuba Orfenova, piano	2:17	8.554357
2	**The Storm, Op. 76 (Conclusion)** Polish National Radio Symphony Orchestra; Antoni Wit	7:01	8.550716
3	**Romance in F minor for piano, Op. 5** Oxana Yablonskaya, piano	6:13	8.553330
4	**Romeo and Juliet (fantasy overture)** National Symphony Orchestra of Ukraine; Theodore Kuchar	20:26	8.555923
5	**To Forget so Soon** Ljuba Kazarnovskays, soprano, Ljuba Orfenova, piano	3:13	8.554357
6	**String Quartet No. 1 in D major, Op. 11** Movement 2: Andante cantabile New Haydn Quartet, Budapest	6:36	8.550847
7	**Symphony No. 2 in C minor, Op. 17 'Little Russian'** Finale: Moderato assai - Allegro vivo Polish National Radio Symphany Orchestra; Adrian Leaper	10:33	8.550488
8	**The Snow Maiden, Op. 12** No. 15: Brusila's Song Elena Okolysheva, mezzo-soprano; Arkady Mishenkin, tenor; Moscow Capella; Moscow Symphony Orchestra; Igor Golovchin	1:33	8.553856
9	**Piano Concerto No. 1 in B flat minor, Op. 23** Finale: Allegro con fuoco Bernd Glemser, piano; Polish National Radio Symphany Orchestra; Antoni Wit	7:10	8.550891
10	**Symphony No. 4 in F minor, Op. 36** Movement 3: Scherzo (Pizzicato ostinato): Allegro - Meno mosso - Tempo I Polish National Radio Symphony Orchestra; Adrian Leaper	5:56	8.550819

[11] **Variations on a Rococo Theme for cello and orchestra, Op. 33 (conclusion)** 2:11
Maria Kliegel, cello; National Symphony Orchestra of Ireland; Gerhard Markson 8.550519

[12] **Eugene Onegin, Op. 24** 6:17
Act II, Scene 2: Lensky's aria 'Where, o where have you gone?'
Vladimir Grishko, tenor; Ukraine State Radio Symphony Orchestra; Vladimir Sirenko 8.554834

TT 79:27

For more information on these tracks, see page 216.

On CD Two

1	**Violin Concerto in D major, Op. 35** Finale: Allegro vivacissimo Takako Nishizaki, violin; Slovak Philharmonic Orchestra; Kenneth Jean	10:46 8.550153
2	**Liturgy of St. John Chrysostom, Op. 41** No. 11: Epiclesis Viktor Ovdiy, tenor; Pavlo Mezhulin, bass; Kiev Chamber Choir; Mykola Hobdych	2:59 8.553854
3	**Capriccio italien, Op. 45 (Conclusion)** National Symphony Orchestra of Ukraine; Theodore Kuchar	4:06 8.555923
4	**1812 (festival overture), Op. 49 (Conclusion)** National Symphony Orchestra of Ukraine; Theodore Kuchar	6:34 8.555923
5	**Serenade in C major, for strings, Op. 48** Movement 2: Valse Vienna Chamber Orchestra; Philippe Entremont	3:57 8.550404
6	**Piano Trio in A minor, Op. 50** Movement 2: Tema con variazioni (Excerpts) Vovka Ashkenazy, piano; Richard Stamper, violin; Christine Jackson, cello	6:55 8.550467
7	**Manfred Symphony, Op. 58** Movement 2: Vivace con spirito Slovak Radio Symphany Orchestra; Ondrej Lenárd	9:44 8.550224
8	**Symphony No. 5 in E minor, Op. 64** Movement 2: Andante cantabile, con alcuna licenza Polish National Radio Symphony Orchestra; Antoni Wit	13:40 8.550716
9	**The Sleeping Beauty, Op. 66** Act I, No. 7: Valse Slovak State Philharmonic Orchestra (Košice); Andrew Mogrelia	4:46 8.550490–92

[10] **The Queen of Spades, Op. 68** 2:49
Act I, Scene 3: Hermann's aria 'Forgive me, heavenly creature'
Vladimir Grishko, tenor; Ukraine State Radio Symphony Orchestra; Vladimir Sirenko 8.554843

[11] **The Nutcracker, Op. 71** 2:17
Act II, No. 14, Variation 2: 'The Dance of the Sugar Plum Fairy'
Slovak Radio Symphony Orchestra; Ondrej Lenárd 8.550324–25

[12] **Symphony No. 6 in B minor, Op. 74 'Pathétique'** 10:51
Act I, No. 7: Valse
Slovak State Philharmonic Orchestra (Košice);
Andrew Mogrelia 8.550490–92

TT 79:23

For more information on these tracks, see page 223.

Preface

I caught the Russian bug in my teens. Voraciously, I devoured the classics of Tolstoy, Dostoyevsky, Gogol, Turgenev and Chekhov in the translations of Constance Garnett. In my twenties, I immersed myself in the Russian language and became gripped by Russian history. Curiously, only latterly was I seized by Russian music, and Tchaikovsky in particular. Hitherto, my Slavic enthusiasms had extended little beyond a near-obsession with Mussorgsky's *Pictures at an Exhibition* and a romanticised love of Russian folk music, which I knew mainly through the seductive recreations of the gypsies. The first recording I ever recall hearing was an old '78' of Feodor Chaliapin, whom I assumed to be at least eight feet tall, singing the 'Volga Boat Song'. The thrill of it lives with me to this day. In my thirties I belatedly discovered the operas of Glinka, and was hooked from the start. Tchaikovsky, though, was a slow burn. Slow but steady. I am a musician of predominantly Germanic proclivities, and not by natural sympathy an opera man, so it was not until my fifties that I discovered *Eugene Onegin* in earnest. That proved to be my gateway into the full range of Tchaikovsky's multicoloured world.

Like many reared in the 1940s and 1950s, I owed the lateness of my Tchaikovskyan epiphany largely to the residue of snobbery. That climate has now changed markedly for the better. Only in the most diehard circles is he still associated with 1950s Hollywood and tacky greetings cards. His status as a great composer, in spite of his indiscriminate popularity, is now more or less universally acknowledged. His personality, however, remains both elusive and controversial, and it is with that, more than with the details of his music (which is nevertheless liberally covered), that this book is primarily concerned. It is not an act of revelation, nor does it masquerade as a work of imposing scholarship. It is envisaged as an introduction to both the man and his work, but it is also approached as a story. Its intended readership is emphatically non-specialist. No previous musical knowledge is assumed, and though the music is discussed at some length I have striven to avoid jargon – and to budget for the inevitable use of a few technical terms, I have ensured that a glossary is ever ready in the wings.

The music is not treated in a separate section of the book, as in the conventional life-and-works format, but rather in a sequence of 'Interludes', alternating with the biographical chapters so that readers can opt, if they wish, to read the chapters as a continuous narrative, turning to the specifically musical discussions later on. The interludes, in any case, are not primarily analytical; they amount to a generically organised survey of Tchaikovsky's output and also include biographical material. They can be read in any order, but they have been organised in such a way as to grow naturally out of the narrative chapters that precede them (which are themselves not without musical commentary).

While avoiding the kind of imaginary scene-setting that blights so many biographies, I have attempted to give the book some of the immediacy of a novel by allowing its protagonists wherever possible to unfurl the story in their own words. These give a far richer and more immediate portrait of both the characters and their time than any amount of subjective 'interpretation'. That said, interpretation is inevitable: the mere selection of quotations is an act of interpretation, before commentary even begins. In a more passive sense, so too is the reader's response to them. There are no absolute truths in biography beyond simple factual accuracy, though in some cases this is difficult if not impossible to determine. I have done my best in this regard.

The advent of the CD was an inestimable blessing to the musical biographer. Where writers on art and literature have long been able to quote in evidence, printing either the original text or pictorial reproductions, writers on music have had to rely on inadequate verbal description, or textual illustrations which most readers may be unable to read, much less hear in their heads. Then along comes the CD, compact as described, which slips easily into the inside covers, and the problem is solved. In the present case, we have decided to include only whole works, movements or self-contained sections, so that the CDs can be listened to not only in conjunction with the text, which is cross-referenced, but purely for pleasure. And expanding the breadth and depth of musical biography still further (indeed immeasurably so) are the almost infinite resources of the Internet. Here whole works by the composer are made available to the reader, as well as music by his contemporaries and immediate forbears. The hope is that text and music will be mutually nourishing, in whatever mixture. The still greater hope is that the book will be an absorbing and entertaining read, enjoyable as well as informative, companionable as well as occasionally provocative, if only of thought. Its cast of characters and the story they have to tell might strain credulity in the cinema, but they represent, as far as can be determined, the truth (though no book – of this or any other size – can lay claim to the whole truth and nothing but the truth). The veracity of the witnesses, however, as in real life, may occasionally be open to doubt.

Chapter 1

Childhood, Boyhood, Youth 1840–1864

Childhood, Boyhood, Youth 1840–1864

A man who conducts with one hand, gripping his chin with the other to keep his head from falling off, could fairly be said to have problems. No one would deny that Pyotr Il'yich Tchaikovsky had problems, least of all the man himself. Their nature and their source, however, remain the stuff of argument. Was he simply a neurotic? A pampered child, gifted or cursed, as the case may be, with genius? Or were his problems genetic? The arguments are nothing new, of course, and are unlikely ever to be finally resolved. Nonetheless, even without a clinically decisive explanation, the life story of this charismatic, tormented, infuriating and lovable human being holds an endless fascination for all who encounter it, just as his music has held the world in thrall throughout the century and more since his death – and even his death is still hotly debated.

In few composers, and still fewer great composers, has the unity of the life and the music been more blatantly, or more defencelessly, obvious. As a man, Tchaikovsky could be devious, insincere and two-faced, though seldom if ever malicious. As a musician he was as honest as they come. It is perhaps the very directness of his music, as much as his prodigious gift for melody and orchestration, that has endeared him to so many millions. He speaks for himself, from himself and of himself, and though mercifully few others have experienced life so intensely as Tchaikovsky he speaks of emotions that are common to all humanity, and universally recognised as such. 'Who hears music,' wrote Robert Browning in 1871, 'has his solitude peopled at once.' Who hears Tchaikovsky's music is always included. For generations he has lessened people's loneliness all over the world. His best music says to the listener: 'Yes. I too have been there. And I have emerged – often triumphantly, sometimes even joyfully. I know your pain; and I know your joy.'

For generations he has lessened people's loneliness all over the world. His best music says 'Yes. I too have been there.

According to legend, Tchaikovsky twice attempted suicide, the second time successfully. We shall have reason to question that legend, but even if true, it does not negate the demonstrable fact that this was a man whose love of life was ultimately very great, and whose capacity not only for love but for sheer enjoyment, even playfulness, could be positively contagious. All this is in the music. It is also in the life.

Like many great stories, Tchaikovsky's begins unremarkably: in the Russian province of Vyatka, in Votkinsk, which was situated on a tributary of the River Kama just west of the Ural mountains. His father, Il'ya Petrovich, was an easy-going, affable man of no great sophistication or intellect; he was an inspector of mines who seems never to have been interesting, let alone stimulating, but he was warmly affectionate, even sentimental. While not a philanderer, he nursed a lifelong love of women that was much remarked on by those who knew him. He had been widowed, and his second wife, Alexandra Andreyevna, was eighteen years his junior and of French extraction. Tall, attractive and notably reserved, she had grown up and been educated in an orphanage, from which she emerged fluent in German and French, modestly cultured, able to play both the piano and the harp, and to sing moderately well. Tchaikovsky had six siblings: an older brother, Nikolay; a

The composer's father, Il'ya Petrovich Tchaikovsky

younger sister, Alexandra (Sasha); a half-sister, Zinaida, by his father's first marriage; and three younger brothers – Ippolit, the eldest, and the twins Anatoly (Tolya) and Modest (pronounced 'Modyest'). At the time of Tchaikovsky's birth in 1840, the family lived, as Modest was later to point out, in circumstances that were more than comfortable:

The composer's mother, Alexandra Andreyevna Tchaikovskaya (née *Assier)*

The position of inspector in the case of such important mines as those of Votkinsk closely resembled that of a wealthy landowner living on his estate. In some respects it was even more advantageous, because he had life's every luxury provided for him: a fine house, a staff of servants, and almost unlimited control over a number of human beings. Il'ya Tchaikovsky even had at his command a small army of a hundred Cossacks, and a little court, consisting of such employees in the mines as had any claim to social position. The fine salary, thanks to the wise economy of his wife, sufficed not only for every comfort, but even admitted of something being put by for less prosperous times.

The house at Votkinsk, where Tchaikovsky spent his childhood years

Among the most prized possessions in this well-appointed household was an orchestrion, one of the earliest and grandest of mass-produced musical machines. A precursor of the gramophone, it brought a wide range of music into many homes where such pieces might otherwise never have been heard, save for the stumbling fingers of children enduring (or in some cases actually enjoying) their obligatory practice time. The music disgorged in the Tchaikovsky home included a wide range of operatic excerpts, most notably arias from Mozart's *Don Giovanni*, closely followed in family popularity by works of Rossini, Bellini and Donizetti. In most households, the orchestrion was a source of pleasure, but for the young Tchaikovsky it was very much more.

Among the earliest vignettes to have entered the mainstream of Tchaikovskyan biography is an account by his French governess, Fanny Dürbach, of entering the nursery one evening to find the tiny child convulsed in tears. His explanation troubled her. 'It's this music!' he cried, 'this music!' She listened, but heard nothing. Pyotr persisted. 'No! No!' He pointed to his head. 'It's here! Here! I can't make it go away. It leaves me no peace!' In a sense it never did go away, and Fanny's recollections of the child Tchaikovsky could be applied, with only minor alterations, to the man he was to become:

> *His sensitivity was infinite. The tiniest thing could disturb or offend him in some way. What would have been the merest trifle to other children affected him very deeply. The question of punishment was unthinkable. Even with scoldings and warnings, the slightest increase of severity would upset him quite alarmingly. He was a child of glass. In dealing with him, one had always to exercise the utmost care.*

Serenity, or anything approaching it, was not so unknown to Tchaikovsky as mythology would have it, but it remained a luxury, the exception rather than the rule. The testimony of his long-time doctor and friend Vasily Bertenson is borne out by others (though there are few who knew him longer or from such a professional perspective): 'As a child, Pyotr Il'yich would often wake up in the middle of the night in hysterical fits. Later on, this translated itself into insomnia and in phenomena that he called "little fits", in which he would suddenly awaken as though from some kind of shock, with a sensation of uncontrollable terror.' Modest confirms that his brother was of

Serenity, or anything approaching it, was not unknown to Tchaikovsky, but it remained a luxury, the exception rather than the rule.

an 'extraordinarily nervous disposition' and likewise speaks of 'fits' and 'frequent hysterics'. He suggests these might have been an inheritance from their maternal grandfather, who suffered similar attacks that (like Dostoyevsky's) were possibly epileptic. There were times, in later life, when the 'little fits' referred to by Bertenson would recur almost nightly, instilling in Tchaikovsky a hatred of going to bed that could afflict him for months on end. During these spells, he would sleep now in an armchair, now on the sofa, but his bed would remain undisturbed. The same could not be said of his mind.

When he was eight, Tchaikovsky's world turned upside down. His father, in the mistaken belief that a better position awaited him elsewhere, resigned from his post, uprooted his family, bade an enforced but reluctant farewell to the beloved Fanny Dürbach and headed for Moscow, despite its then being in the grip of a cholera epidemic. The hoped-for job did not materialise. Without a breadwinner and fearful of infection, the family now decamped to St Petersburg. Here, Pyotr and Nikolay were entrusted to the unsympathetic care of their half-sister Zinaida (herself, in Modest's words, 'still half a child') before being enrolled at a boarding school, where they were treated severely, criminally overworked, and surrounded by 'a host of boys who received them with the customary thumps and whacks'. The nervousness of Pyotr's disposition intensified. His 'little fits' worsened; he grew listless, irritable, argumentative – quite unlike his former self. In December, both brothers came down with measles. Nikolay recovered according to the usual pattern, but Pyotr did not. He suffered a series of increasingly violent attacks and the doctors diagnosed a spinal disorder, though they must have reconsidered as we hear no more about it. All work, however, was forbidden, and

Tchaikovsky's father uprooted his family and headed for Moscow, despite its then being in the grip of a cholera epidemic.

for six months Pyotr lived the life of an invalid. As he returned to something like normality, he spent much of his time at the piano, which he apparently mastered with relative ease.

In the spring of 1849, Il'ya at last secured another job, as manager of a provincial ore mine. Thus the family was again uprooted. They returned to the Urals, but not to Votkinsk. Alapayevsk was a remote, predominantly working-class community, far removed from the cultured sophistication of St Petersburg. Increasingly, from this time onwards, especially in the absence of his brother, who was now at a different boarding school, music became the young Tchaikovsky's principal distraction from the sorrows of his daily life. Though not yet ten, he was imbued with a degree of nostalgia unusual in one so young. At eight he had written to Fanny: 'We have been here for almost a month now, and every day we all think of you; we are so sad. But I mustn't recall our life in Votkinsk; I can't help crying when I think of it.' Only at the piano, he confessed to her, could he be truly happy.

Music became the young Tchaikovsky's principal distraction from the sorrows of his daily life.

With music, Tchaikovsky escaped into a new kind of reality, which he could shape and order as he pleased. He was perceived as musical but outclassed as a pianist by his elder brother, whose praises were sung louder than his own – not least by their mother, whom Pyotr adored to distraction. It was never envisaged by anyone, however, that either boy would become a professional musician. Indeed Russian culture at that time exalted the amateur over the professional. Music conservatoires had no place, and even Glinka, 'the father of Russian music', had been an amateur. So, strictly speaking, were Balakirev (a university-trained mathematician), Borodin (a distinguished chemist), Mussorgsky (an undistinguished military and government official) and Rimsky-Korsakov (a naval officer).

In the summer of 1850, it was decided that Pyotr, then aged ten, should be enrolled in the preparatory division of the St Petersburg School of Jurisprudence, an institution renowned for its discipline, and which was originally founded to improve the status of the lesser aristocracy. The intention was to cure his apathy, reverse his tendency to listlessness, and prepare him for a respectable career in the civil service or the military. Before depositing her son and departing for home, his mother took him to the opera, for a performance of Glinka's *A Life for the Tsar.* It was one of the highpoints of his life. But the joy that sprang from this occasion (unlike his love of the opera) was short-lived. To the end of his days, he could never recall his mother's departure without a tremor of horror: 'It was the most powerful grief I had ever experienced. Every minute of that terrible day is etched in my memory as though it were yesterday.' In the words of one eyewitness:

His mother took him to a performance of Glinka's *A Life for the Tsar.* It was one of the highpoints of his life.

> *When the moment of parting arrived, Tchaikovsky lost all self-control. Clinging wildly to his mother, he refused to let her go. No kisses, no comforting words, no promises of a speedy return were of any avail. He heard nothing, saw nothing, and seemed to merge as one with his venerated mother. It became necessary to drag the poor child away and hold him fast until his mother had driven off. Even then, he broke loose, and with a cry of despair, ran after the carriage, trying to seize hold of it in the doomed hope of bringing it to a stop. Fully thirty years later he affirmed that he could never pass that way again without feeling afresh the resentment and mad despair that had seized him as the carriage bearing everything dearest to his heart slipped out of sight.*

The School of Jurisprudence was originally an enlightened, even humane institution, described by one distinguished former pupil as 'redolent, to some degree, of home, and family life,' but in 1850, when Tchaikovsky arrived, it had undergone a drastic transformation. It had just been entirely refashioned after an edict of Tsar Nicholas I that imposed strict military discipline on the entire imperial school system. The regime was now harsh, the accommodation spartan and communal, affording little in the way of privacy, and bullying was rife, indeed almost institutionalised. The tools of discipline included public flogging, carried out in the compulsory presence of both junior and senior pupils as well as teachers and staff. It was a spectacle that no one forgot, let alone someone of Tchaikovsky's sensibilities. Years later, the eminent critic Vladimir Stasov remembered one such occasion with bitter vividness:

> *The director yelled and threatened at the top of his voice, losing all control and working himself up to a point of such hysteria that he determined to whip the entire class. The boys were lined up, and the punishment began. Two soldiers seized hold of Spassky, the boy at the end, who resisted, vainly fighting back in desperation. They stripped him naked, laid him on a bench and whipped him without mercy. The director paced back and forth with faltering steps, holding his hands behind his back, while the teachers, as required, maintained official silence. After Spassky, they flogged Vletlitsky, a well-known mischief-maker in general, but in this case quite blameless. As the whipping continued, he kept crying out, in the most heartrending voice, that he was innocent. Our insides trembled. At last, the director called a halt and left the room without another word or a backward glance. We dispersed and retreated in silence to our quarters.*

On another occasion, one of Tchaikovsky's friends was caught smoking. He was sentenced by Colonel Rutenberg, the much-feared Inspector of Students, to sixty-five strokes of the birch. Witnessing this savagery, a classmate and later a friend of Tchaikovsky's, a little boy called Maslov, became almost hysterical and burst into sobs. Rutenberg threatened to lay him out there and then and flog him too. The sobbing ceased, and the punishment continued.

These grisly rituals traumatised many of those who were forced to observe them. How the supersensitive Tchaikovsky contrived to remain silent would be difficult to understand but for one overriding factor: unbeknownst to any of the authorities, he too smoked. It was a habit he retained to the end of his life. And there were other addictions, likewise acquired at the school. As he reflected many years later:

> *It is said that to abuse oneself with drink is harmful. I entirely agree. Yet it is a poison I can't do without. I now get drunk every night, and cannot do otherwise. In the first stage of drunkenness, I feel a great happiness. I comprehend so much more than when I'm sober. And in truth, I haven't noticed that my health suffers much.*

He was possessed of a robust constitution, and like many of his countrymen could consume an inordinate amount of alcohol.

Nor did it. Though a confirmed and self-confessed hypochondriac, he was possessed of a robust constitution, and like many of his countrymen he could consume an inordinate amount of alcohol and appear quite unaffected.

Had Rutenberg known about either of these habits, then the least of Tchaikovsky's concerns would have been his health. But he never did find out. And almost uniquely amongst the boys, Tchaikovsky was never flogged, nor ever threatened with a flogging. As one of his schoolmates recalled:

'There was definitely something special about him, even then – something that separated him from the rest of us and made our hearts go out to him. Kindness, generosity, a keen responsiveness to others and a curious light-heartedness about himself were characteristic of his personality in those days. Even the unspeakable Rutenberg seemed to feel a special sympathy for him.'

Of the thirty-nine letters written by Tchaikovsky to his family from the school, there is not one in which he speaks disapprovingly of anyone, or without praise and appreciation. On the basis of his letters alone, it would appear that all those around him were unfailingly affectionate, attentive and kind, and worthy of nothing but love and gratitude. His nature, by all accounts, was almost disturbingly affectionate, compassionate and, above all, unjudging. Either that, or his powers of suppression at that age were greater than his outpourings in later life would suggest. In the light of his handling of Rutenberg, this possibility should not be ruled out.

'I can never be reconciled to the idea that my mother, that most beautiful person, whom I loved beyond words, is utterly extinguished.'

Tchaikovsky's greatest crisis during these years came with the death of his mother from cholera in 1854. She was forty-one; he was fourteen. As he wrote, more than two decades later: 'Despite all the strengths of my convictions, I can never be reconciled to the idea that my mother, that most beautiful person, whom I loved beyond words, is utterly extinguished and that I shall never have the opportunity of telling her that after twenty-three years, my love for her burns as powerfully as ever.' A frequent witness to this unresolved bereavement was his brother Modest: 'He would often recall the unearthly happiness he experienced as he pressed himself to her breast after three or four months of not seeing her. Many years after he had attained full maturity, he could never speak of her without tears coming to his eyes. Those around him would therefore be careful to avoid the subject.'

In the immediate aftermath of his mother's death – Tchaikovsky's only solace was in music.

Throughout these testing times, Tchaikovsky's musical gifts grew more obvious almost by the day; but still nobody, including himself, gave even a passing thought to his pursuing a musical career. He received no encouragement at the school, either from the staff or even, surprisingly, from his fellow students. As one of them put it: 'Of his future glory, we had not an inkling.' For nine years, he remained at the School of Jurisprudence, following the path laid out for him by his parents. In the immediate aftermath of his mother's death – as after that first separation from her – Tchaikovsky's only solace was in music. Now, however, he did not merely play it, for he was beginning seriously to compose it. Within a short time, he began sounding like a true professional, producing mostly songs, but songs of real flair and atmosphere (such as **Zemfira's Song**). Given his continuing lack of local celebrity, most strikingly at school, one can only suppose that he kept the fruits of these early efforts a tightly guarded secret. These, then, were the circumstances in which Tchaikovsky coped with the intrinsic tensions and uncertainties of adolescence – defined, as ever, by the awakening, both physical and psychological, of sexuality as a definitive if not dominant aspect of self.

The origins of sexual orientation in the development of human personality are as speculative as the precise relationship of genetics and environment. Few would dispute, however, that it is in adolescence that patterns of sexual behaviour evolve, without necessarily determining the proclivities of adulthood. As at most single-sex boarding schools for teenagers, homosexual activity was commonplace at the School of Jurisprudence – it ranged from relatively innocent experimentation to cynical and heavy-handed seduction. Although particularly vulnerable to influence in the aftermath of his mother's death, Tchaikovsky had long been a natural focus for homosexual attention. As described by one adoring schoolmate, Alexander Mikhaylov, 'he was always pensive, preoccupied with something or other. With a slight but charming smile, and girlishly pretty, he would appear among us in his little jacket, with the sleeves rolled up, and spend hours on end at the piano in the music room.'

He exuded throughout his life an almost dangerous charm, felt equally by men and women.

Tchaikovsky's 'prettiness' was much remarked upon from early childhood. With his 'angelic' disposition, his manifest sensitivity and his gentle humour, he exuded throughout his life an almost dangerous charm, felt equally by men and women. Craving approbation, and not strong-willed, he was both sensually inclined and sometimes disconcertingly compliant. At the School of Jurisprudence, he came under the influence of a thriving homosexual subculture, whose most striking member was also his closest and most intensely admired friend, the future poet Alexey Apukhtin, who in his youth was regarded by many as a second Pushkin. From the time of his arrival in Tchaikovsky's class to the moment of their graduation (this we learn from Modest, corroborated by others), 'Apukhtin played an enormous role in Pyotr Il'yich's life,' not least as a sexual role model.

Following his graduation in 1859, and as envisaged from the start, Tchaikovsky took a job in the Ministry of Justice, where he made new friends. Despite his self-acknowledged shyness he made friends easily – though he persistently denied this – and he enjoyed a rich and varied social life. That special something noted by his contemporaries at the School of Jurisprudence had not abandoned him. As one friend put it, adding his voice to a host of others:

Tchaikovsky in 1859, the year in which he graduated from the School of Jurisprudence and began working at the Ministry of Justice

> *It was quite impossible not to love him. Everything, from his youthful appearance to his wonderful, penetrating gaze, made him irresistibly attractive. What struck one most of all, however, was his gentle modesty, and his conspicuous kindness. No one else could treat everyone so cordially; none other possessed his childlike, pure, and optimistic view of people. Everyone felt, when conversing with him, a special warmth and caress in the sound of his voice, in his words, and in his expression.*

Behind this charm and apparent pleasure in conviviality, however, there lurked a typically Russian, quiet, almost lazy fatalism very much in accord with the Romantic temper of the times.

To his habitual use of tobacco and alcohol was now added another weakness, which like the others never left him, and of which he himself was constantly aware:

> *When I have money in my pocket, I invariably squander it on pleasures. That this is both dishonourable and foolish, I know full well, of course. I have huge debts to settle, and major necessities to which I should attend. Yet such is my lack of moral strength that I knowingly turn my back on these, abandoning myself wholly to enjoyment. Such is my character. I am well aware that sooner or later (and probably sooner) I shall lose what strength I have to struggle with the challenges of life and shall probably smash myself to pieces. Until then, however, I enjoy life as best I can and seek out pleasure at whatever cost.*

Tchaikovsky in this vein must not be taken at face value. It seems at times as if by self-chastisement he somehow absolves himself – like those who believe that in apologising they discharge their debt to the affronted. Had Tchaikovsky truly abandoned himself to hedonism, the reactions of his fellows would hardly have been what they were. His 'angelic' aura was not a pose; yet Modest concurs with his brother's self-portrait, and amplifies it: 'In the first years after his graduation from the school, he remained the former adolescent schoolboy. The same insatiable thirst for merriment, the same insouciant pursuit of pleasure, the superficial view of life, all remained as much a part of him in his liberty as they had been at school.'

Nevertheless, in the early spring of 1861 we get the first signs that music was beginning to get the upper hand. In a letter to his sister on 10 March, he reports:

> *My musical talent was discussed at dinner. Papa insists it's not too late for me to become an artist. But the fact is that even if I do have some talent, it probably is too late to develop it properly. They have made a clerk out of me, and a poor one at that: I try to improve as much as I can, to take my work more seriously – but now I study thoroughbass as well!*

The possibility of abandoning law in favour of music as his profession moved to the top of his agenda.

In the course of the next two years, the possibility of abandoning law in favour of music as his profession moved steadily closer to the top of his agenda. In 1862 he supplemented his study of thoroughbass by enrolling in a class at the Russian Musical Society. This establishment, one year later, became the St Petersburg Conservatoire under the directorship of Anton Rubinstein, perhaps the greatest Russian pianist of the nineteenth century as well as a noted composer. Rubinstein encouraged him to take the plunge, and in 1863 Tchaikovsky resigned from his post at the Ministry and became a full-time student of the Conservatoire at the late age of twenty-three.

For all his charm and modesty, and his much-remarked generosity of spirit, Tchaikovsky was a man of strong opinions. As his friend Herman Laroche observed:

> *During this period, Pyotr Il'yich had a great many unhealthy musical antipathies. These related not just to composers but to whole genres of composition – or more exactly, to their sound. Thus, for instance, he disliked the sound of the piano with orchestra, the sound of a string quartet or quintet, and most of all the sound of the piano in combination with one or several stringed instruments. Not just once, nor ten times, nor a hundred, did I hear from him what was almost an oath: that he would never compose a single piano concerto, or a single sonata for violin and piano, or a single trio, quartet, and so on. Stranger still was his pledge at around this time never to compose either short piano pieces or romances* [songs].

His First Piano Concerto is among the most popular ever written.

Those particular aversions he overcame. His First Piano Concerto is among the most popular ever written, his string quartets (one of which moved Tolstoy to tears) have enjoyed unbroken popularity, and his Piano Trio has never been out of the repertoire. The same goes for a number of his many short piano pieces, and hardly fewer songs. His tastes in composers, however, never wavered. From early childhood, Mozart was his highest point of reference:

> *I love Mozart as a musical Christ. It should be noted, I think, that he lived to about the same age as Christ. I find no sacrilege in this comparison. Mozart was such an angelic creature, of such childlike purity. His music is suffused with a beauty so unattainably sublime that if anyone can be mentioned in the same breath as Christ then it is certainly*

> *Mozart. It is my absolute conviction that in Mozart we reach the most exalted peak of perfection that musical beauty has attained. No one has such a power to make me weep, to tremble with rapture from the knowledge that I am close to something that we can truly call the ideal.*

When it came to other composers, Tchaikovsky's antipathies were at least as forthright as his enthusiasms, and in most cases they lasted him a lifetime:

> *The other day I played over the music of that scoundrel Brahms. What a giftless bastard! It irritates me that this self-inflated mediocrity is hailed as a genius. In comparison to Brahms, even Raff is a giant, not to speak of Rubinstein, who is after all a live and important human being, while Brahms is a chaos of utterly empty dried-up tripe!*

At that time, the musical world was divided between two opposing camps, the Brahmsians and the Wagnerites. It was an absurd over-simplification, and to Tchaikovsky an irrelevance. After visiting Wagner's stronghold at Bayreuth, he wrote, tersely:

> *Wagner's* Rheingold *has been performed: as a scenic spectacle the work was interesting enough, and I was fascinated because of the astounding production; musically, however, it's really an incredible mess, though not without an occasional flash of some beautiful or striking detail. At least I wasn't bored, but no one could possibly say that I enjoyed myself.*

And Bach?

> *I like playing Bach from time to time, because it's always*

interesting to play a good fugue – but I really cannot regard him, like some, as a great genius.

Handel?

Handel strikes me as so fourth-rate that he's not even interesting.

Beethoven?

Beethoven's middle period is all right, and some of the first period, but I positively loathe the last period, particularly the late quartets. There are certainly flashes there – but certainly not more than that.

At least Tchaikovsky is more generous than Tolstoy, who flatly declared that 'Beethoven had no talent' even though he was generally regarded throughout the nineteenth century as the greatest composer who ever lived.

Tchaikovsky's own composing gained steadily in fluency and invention but his genius took a long time to surface. Of all his student works, only one gave any real indication of the riches to come. If his other compositions were competent but rather anonymous, his orchestral overture to Ostrovsky's play **The Storm** reveals for the first time his distinctive personality as a composer. It also reveals a very Russian one. But he was not without competition.

Interlude I:
Tchaikovsky at the Piano

Tchaikovsky, like Mozart, Beethoven, Chopin and Brahms, wrote piano works throughout his professional life. That is where, on the whole, any similarity ends, for while these other composers continually developed, exploring new realms of pianism and emotional experience alike, Tchaikovsky did neither. His best keyboard works are not inconsiderable (though none is a milestone in musical-pianistic history), but the great majority of them are salon miniatures specifically aimed at the booming domestic market, for no single instrument has ever dominated a century of music-making as the piano did the nineteenth. That said, most of Tchaikovsky's pieces were of a polished professionalism seldom encountered elsewhere in the ubiquitous 'Young Lady Albums' compiled in vast numbers on both sides of the Atlantic. Many, especially from his last set, Op. 72, are also of biographical interest in that they were written for, and dedicated to, his numerous piano-playing friends and colleagues. They amount, in varying degrees, to pen portraits of the recipients. Many more have the twin advantages of being both enjoyable, even delightful, to play, while not requiring any great technical prowess.

Tchaikovsky wrote piano works throughout his professional life.

Long before he formally composed for the piano, Tchaikovsky played the instrument with enthusiasm and facility, and showed an exceptional ability to improvise on any given theme. By the time he began his long stint at the St Petersburg School of Jurisprudence, he showed much more than mere promise as a pianist, yet surprisingly, apart from successfully entertaining his family and friends, he never caused much of a stir. We have a partial explanation in the testimony of Herman Laroche – all the more surprising considering the often extreme emotionalism of Tchaikovsky's own music:

He showed much more than mere promise as a pianist, yet surprisingly, he never caused much of a stir.

> *Generally speaking, he played the piano very well: boldly, even brilliantly, and could manage pieces of quite eye-popping difficulty. At the same time, his playing was strangely rough, and lacking in warmth and deep emotion – exactly the reverse of what you might suppose. But the fact is that Pyotr Il'yich had a horror of sentimentality, again surprising. He deplored excessively 'expressive' piano playing, and often made fun of other composers' exhortations to 'play with feeling.' His own musical sentiments, I would say, were characterised even by a certain chasteness, and his fear of vulgarity could drive him to the opposite extreme.*

We get another glimpse of this, in a non-pianistic context, through a remark made by Tchaikovsky himself, many years later, with reference to one of his closest friends: 'I went with Apukhtin to bid farewell [to one of their female society acquaintances]. He presented her with some verses and was so overcome with emotion that he began to sob. I cannot abide such vulgarities.' And this from one of the most chronically lachrymose adults in history.

Despite his reverence for Mozart, Tchaikovsky could never really get on with Classical sonata form. He gave the name 'sonata' to only two works in his entire output, both of them for the piano. Though its misleadingly high opus number might suggest otherwise, the Sonata in C sharp minor, Op. 80 of 1865 is actually the earlier work. Most of the few musicians who know it also find it the more interesting of the two. The second, the so-called 'Grand' Sonata in G, Op. 37 of 1878, is a big, rather pretentious concert piece, favoured by enough virtuosos to keep it in the repertoire but described by the composer himself as a 'rather dry and complicated piece.' It has its ardent supporters to this day, but many confirmed Tchaikovskyans side with his own description and regard it as one of the dullest and least pleasing pieces he ever wrote. Both works, like quite a number of his less imposing structures, show up one of his abiding liabilities as a piano composer, namely his tendency to treat the instrument as a surrogate orchestra. Liszt and Beethoven did likewise, though Liszt, in particular, had an idiomatic grasp of pianistic textures exceeded only, if even then, by Chopin's.

The most pervasive influence on Tchaikovsky's piano writing was unquestionably Schumann, a fact that he implicitly acknowledged when naming his Op. 39 collection *Album for Children* (after Schumann's well-known *Album for the Young*). These twenty-four 'easy pieces' (with specifically 'national' numbers evoking Germany, Bohemia, Poland, France, Italy and of course Russia) amount to a delightful and unassuming musical travelogue, a kind of storybook-cum-picture-gallery anthology, featuring predatory witches, marching soldiers, larks a-trilling, fairy-tales a-chilling, and so forth. Here, Schumann's restless lyricism, the sheer range of his ideas and his penchant for ingenious rhythms exercised a tremendous influence on Tchaikovsky. Unfortunately, so did Schumann's tendency to rhythmic obsession (particularly where dotted rhythms are concerned),

Schumann's restless lyricism, sheer range of ideas and penchant for ingenious rhythms exercised a tremendous influence on Tchaikovsky.

sectional repetitiousness and rather four-square phrasing.

The ghost of Schumann hovers, too, over much of *The Seasons,* Op. 37b, composed in 1876. Probably Tchaikovsky's best-known and most played piano work, it consists of twelve movements ostensibly (though not very obviously) evoking subjects and activities typical of the twelve months from January to December. It was an unashamed potboiler, written in installments, on a regular monthly basis, for the journal *Nouvelliste,* and Tchaikovsky's servant often had to remind him to get on with the task in hand. Treated as a proper cycle, it fails really to cohere. Indeed, except in the hands of a very exceptional pianist, it tends towards monotony when presented whole, whether in recital or on record. In isolation, several of the 'months' have achieved considerable popularity. These include 'At the Fireside' (January), The 'Song of the Lark' (March) – a beautiful *Andante espressivo* in G minor – 'Snowdrops' (April), 'Clear Nights' (May) and 'Troika Ride' (November).

The Seasons consists of twelve movements ostensibly evoking subjects and activities typical of the twelve months from January to December.

The *Twelve Pieces of Moderate Difficulty,* Op. 40, are mostly pretty insipid but include a few that have weathered several generations, most notably the 'Chanson triste', the 'Valse in A flat', the two Russian pieces 'Au village' and 'Danse russe' (a reworking of the more famous dance of the same name in *Swan Lake*), and the last piece of all, the 'Rêverie interrompue'.

Tchaikovsky's swan song where the piano is concerned is the set of *Eighteen Pieces,* Op. 72, each one dedicated to a different friend or colleague (some of whom where stunning virtuosos). None of his earlier sets has anything like the variety of this one, where pieces of near-beginner simplicity stand cheek by jowl with large-scale showstoppers fit to make the greatest pianist sweat. A (very) few brave souls have presented the set complete in concert, but like *The Seasons* it is best sampled in small doses.

Tchaikovsky's piano room at Klin, where he chose to spend his summers from 1885 onwards

Most sets are remembered today by one or two items that have escaped to live a life of their own. Among these are the remarkable and extended 'Theme and Variations in F major' from the *Six Pieces*, Op. 19 (1873), which give us the Tchaikovsky of that period at his most commanding (albeit with Schumann looking conspicuously over his shoulder). This work enjoyed great popularity among pianists in the past and was frequently performed by such luminaries as Hans von Bülow and Emil Gilels, but few of today's players follow their example. Other escapees include the once hugely popular Humoresque in G (the second of the *Two Pieces*, Op. 10), which rose to stardom thanks to a number of orchestrations, one by Leopold Stokowski.

Among the one-offs that remain, many pieces are negligible but some are certainly not. The vaguely Chopinesque **Romance in F minor**, Op. 5, may not be

CD 1
track 3
www.naxosbooks.com

top-drawer Tchaikovsky but it quickly established itself as one of his most popular piano pieces. *Dumka*, Op. 59, is a substantial, imposing work – alternately haunting and scintillating, and requiring a good deal of technique to bring off – but it is not merely a bravura showpiece. Nor should pianists overlook the bold, experimental *Six Pieces on a Single Theme*, Op. 21, written for Tchaikovsky's most intimidating mentor, Anton Rubinstein. Here the spirit of Schumann combines with a near-Bachian mastery of counterpoint and a transformational approach to variation that puts the decorative formulas of the eighteenth century in the shade. While it may fairly be said that much of Tchaikovsky's piano music has earned its neglect, this work emphatically has not.

The bold, experimental *Six Pieces on a Single Theme* was written for Tchaikovsky's most intimidating mentor, Anton Rubinstein.

Also unjustly neglected, despite their many rewards for amateur pianists, are the piano-duet arrangements of *Fifty Russian Folksongs* (1868–9), which are drawn largely from collections by Konstantin Villebois and Balakirev. Many of these are easy and fun to play, and in some cases have the added charm of familiarity since a number of the tunes also crop up in Tchaikovsky's best-known orchestral, chamber and operatic works.

Chapter 2

Coming of Age
1865–1876

Coming of Age
1865–1876

In view of the brash, apparent self-confidence of Tchaikovsky's pronouncements on the great composers, the apparent self-confidence of his music should come as no surprise. Nor should the almost exhibitionist intensity of feeling in a lot of it. As the daughter of one of his closest friends recalled: 'Everyone knew how powerfully his emotions affected him. If he was deeply touched by something, it took him over altogether; his reason then became possessed.'

His fears in particular were obsessive, and at times so irrational that it was then easy, both for outsiders and himself, to question his sanity. It was at his debut as a conductor, at the Conservatoire, aged twenty-five, that he directed the entire performance with his right hand alone and used his left to keep his head on. With signs like that it came as no surprise when, less than a year later, he succumbed to a major nervous breakdown brought on by obsessive overwork on his First Symphony and its attendant anxieties. As Modest reported:

Tchaikovsky succumbed to a major nervous breakdown brought on by obsessive overwork on his First Symphony.

> *In July, he suffered attacks the likes of which were never to recur. The doctor called in to treat him declared him to be 'but a step away from madness' and initially regarded his*

case as almost desperate. The chief symptoms, and certainly the most terrible, were the tormenting hallucinations, which so terrified the victim that he lost all sensation in his arms and legs, which became completely paralysed.

Happily, he made a good recovery, and later that year passed seamlessly from student to teacher. Even before Tchaikovsky graduated from the St Petersburg Conservatoire, Nikolay Rubinstein (a musician and pianist regarded by some as the equal of his more famous elder brother, Anton) had offered him a teaching post at the newly formed Moscow Conservatoire, of which he himself was the dynamic, if somewhat eccentric, director. Thus in January 1866, Tchaikovsky moved from St Petersburg to Moscow, and from one Rubinstein to another. The latter transition proved the more difficult, for Rubinstein insisted on Tchaikovsky's moving in with him. He lavished more care and attention on his new colleague than Tchaikovsky would have liked and swept him up in a whirl of conviviality that the shy composer did not find naturally congenial, even though it came as second nature to Rubinstein. At the same time we should be under no illusions as to the nature and character of that shyness which, though perfectly genuine, was far from absolute.

So much is made of Tchaikovsky's depressive tendencies (not least by himself) that one easily overlooks what is now referred to as the 'bipolar' nature of his condition, and with it, the opposite pole. Even when both are considered, however, perception may still be distorted. Bipolarity is no less jargonistic than 'manic depression', its former popular label, but it is at least more neutral. While 'depression' tends to connote mainly sadness, melancholia and pessimism, the term 'manic', which derives from 'mania' (innocently defined as 'an irrational but irresistible motive for a belief or action'),

Much is made of Tchaikovsky's depressive tendencies.

easily connotes in the popular imagination the frightening image of the 'maniac', the dangerous psychotic. Whether a bipolar disposition in itself constitutes illness at all is a moot point, yet Tchaikovsky has been widely portrayed as a stereotypical 'mad' Russian. This deserves our attention. If we are to gain even a modest understanding of Tchaikovsky the man, we must understand the basics of his particular affliction.

Tchaikovsky has been widely portrayed as a stereotypical 'mad' Russian. This deserves our attention.

Any mental state, sufficiently exaggerated, may sensibly be diagnosed as illness, but the illness lies in the extent of the exaggeration rather than the parent state of mind. The fact is that many (possibly most) highly creative people are subject to considerable mood swings, yet few of them are mentally 'ill', let alone mad. Consider the effects of our two poles as experienced in normal life. When people (bipolar or otherwise) are depressed, the natural impulse is to withdraw. Depression and conviviality are not born soulmates, whereas depression and low self-esteem are. Joy, stimulation, productivity and happiness, on the other hand of euphoria, produce a relative lack of inhibition, and in many people even a degree of innocent, if sometimes socially trying, exhibitionism.

While depression is not by any means a necessary feature of shyness, transient shyness is often a feature of depression. There is no magic or rocket science here, just common sense and logic. Depression begets a lack of confidence, a loss of self-esteem, a draining of energy, a fear of rejection, of disapproval, of being misunderstood. One result? Shyness – as a generally temporary by-product of a particular circumstance. Another result? Loss of perspective; an inclination to interpret things negatively. Thus we find Tchaikovsky writing (in 1867, but it might have been any year):

> *I have made an inner vow never again to spend the summer in places where people dance virtually every day and call on one another every minute . . . But here's the horrid bit: I have become convinced that I harbour within me the disease called 'misanthropy.' I am sometimes overcome by the most frightful fits of hatred toward humanity at large.*

And again, another time, another place, another pretext:

> *In general, I hate mankind, and would gladly escape into the desert with only the most meagre retinue.*

At other times, to other people, he would temper this perception. To Nadezhda von Meck, for instance, in 1879: 'If I am a misanthrope, it is not in the sense of actually hating people but in that of finding their company wearisome.' This can arise from two quite different sources, both of them central features of Tchaikovsky's temperament. People's company is easily wearisome to those whose present state of mind makes even the minimum of social intercourse a major challenge to the will. To communicate at all can be an effort in such circumstances. Through the necessary exercise of will, however, victims of depression often become accomplished dissemblers. The act, when successful, necessarily conceals the effort behind it. What is wearisome is not the person being addressed but precisely the effort required to respond to this person's 'company', which is experienced not as 'companionship' but as a 'presence' that demands a response. Tchaikovsky was right in such circumstances to absolve himself of 'misanthropy.'

At the other extreme – the other extreme of normal, that is to say 'non-ill', life – the experience of company as 'wearisome' is particularly acute when the creative imagination is in full flow, when the requirements of etiquette, even of basic good manners, can be not only irksome but seriously, even 'fatally', distracting. A classic case in point is the 'person from Porlock', whose arrival at Coleridge's door when he was in the throes of creating *Kubla Khan* strangled at birth what might have been one of the greatest epics in English verse. There can be few creative artists in any medium who have not at one time or another had their 'Porlock' experience. This again is distinct from misanthropy.

It is a matter of historical record that Tchaikovsky inspired love and devotion with almost alarming ease.

Whether 'misanthropic' or 'shy', it is a matter of historical record that throughout his life Tchaikovsky inspired love and devotion with almost alarming ease, and to a great extent, he also reciprocated. Our present witness is Vasily Bertenson:

> *Some say Pyotr Il'yich was a misanthrope, but was this really the case? True, he often avoided people, feeling most comfortable in solitude – so much so that even people as close as his sister and brothers could feel burdensome to him; true, too, that he was often happiest when he had no one's company but his servants. Yet this frequently arose not in fact from a dislike of people, but quite the opposite, from a surfeit of love for them. He wanted nothing but the best for everyone, and it seemed sometimes as though he could experience true happiness only when he had succeeded in making someone else happy, or in helping someone, or creating something beautiful.*

It was consequently his living nightmare that he himself might be burdensome to them. This, too, is a classic symptom of depression. In Tchaikovsky's case, however, there was also the quite specific, rational and realistic fear that even rumours of his way of life might cause suffering for those he loved.

Closely related to the (often intermittent) shyness of creative artists, particularly those, like writers and composers, who must create in solitude, is the stock figure of the depressive comedian. This is the entertainer who brings joy and laughter to others while suffering agonies himself, the clown who wants to play Hamlet; the unbuttoned showman, whose ostensibly ironic shyness derives from a lack of self-esteem – or of self-confidence, which is perhaps not quite the same thing. He too is a much misunderstood phenomenon. There is no irony here. The actor, lacking confidence that he will be loved for himself, takes on the role of entertainer both as a mask and as a means of eliciting not only approval, but also the public demonstration of it. The 'egotism' of performers is legendary. Shyness and social or theatrical exhibitionism are often two sides of the same coin. No one enjoys the storytelling of a born raconteur more than the raconteur himself. That indeed is the main secret of his success. Tchaikovsky had this too. Like most of us, he craved approbation, he loved applause. We see an unfamiliar but not untypical side of him in an anecdote from his friend Ivan Klimenko, recounting an adventure on a railway journey:

Tchaikovsky, like most of us, craved approbation, loved applause.

> *Petya began playing about, and doing take-offs of ballet recitatives (he did this wonderfully well), striking all kinds of ballet poses, and then suddenly said to us: 'Gentlemen, would you like me to dance the mazurka before the ladies in the next compartment?' Before anyone could reply, he began, with exaggerated passion, to sing the mazurka from [Glinka's]* A Life for the Tsar *and dashed boldly, and with an 'inspired' face, into the neighbouring compartment, danced the mazurka, afterwards saying 'pardon' to the ladies, before turning his back on them and returning to us, with the same mazurka, keeping a completely serious expression on his face the while. Then, of course, he joined in our quite helpless laughter.*

Such antics, and there are many similar stories, put his much-vaunted shyness in a revealing light. In this mood, and especially when assuming amusing guises, he was far from shy.

Though his early Moscow period set the seal on Tchaikovsky's homosexual lifestyle, there is no reason to suspect Nikolay Rubinstein's motives in taking him in and to a considerable extent taking him over: as Tchaikovsky reported to his brothers, 'Rubinstein looks after me like a proper nanny. Today he forcibly presented me with six new shirts!' The man was conspicuously, even strenuously, heterosexual, and commonly had several students living at his home. Solicitous for his new lodger's career, Rubinstein introduced him to the most powerful men in Russia's musical world (excepting, of course, his brother, whose influence had already made its mark). Of these, Nikolay himself was in many ways the most useful, either conducting or playing in the first performances of many of Tchaikovsky's works, very nearly to the end of his cruelly curtailed life (he died in 1881 at the age of only forty-five). It had been Nikolay who encouraged, almost forced, Tchaikovsky to write his First Symphony, which after its troubled birth and several postponements had its successful first performance in February 1868.

Tchaikovsky's enthusiastic reception was hardly confined to audiences. As recounted by one friend: 'His popularity increased not daily but hourly. Everyone who joined his circle fell under his spell at once. By the start of the '68–'69 season, he was already one of Moscow's greatest favourites, not only as a composer but also as a person.'

'His popularity increased not daily but hourly. Everyone who joined his circle fell under his spell at once'.

Long after recovering from his breakdown, however, Tchaikovsky remained as highly strung and impressionable as the child described by Fanny Dürbach, and his fragility and mercurial temperament could be both disconcerting and alarming. Few attending the successful premiere of his First Symphony would have imagined the scene described by the baritone Konstantin de Lazari after a visit to the zoological gardens in Berlin. On seeing a rabbit devoured by a giant boa constrictor, 'Tchaikovsky let out a terrible cry. He burst into uncontrollable sobs and became completely hysterical. We had no alternative but to return him to the hotel, where it was a long time before we were able to calm him down. Until evening he remained in a feverish condition and could eat nothing at all.'

Tchaikovsky was now twenty-eight. His homosexual lifestyle was well established, and though he pursued it with characteristic circumspection it was evidently untainted by any sense of guilt. Nor did he invariably equate sexual activity with romantic attachment. He was an unashamed sensualist, and serenely promiscuous with it. He also harboured the belief that he could easily become bisexual, as a matter of simple choice, but he had never evinced the slightest romantic, let alone sexual, interest in any girl or woman. In 1868, however, he considerably surprised himself, and all but a few who knew him well, by falling in love with the visiting Belgian opera singer Désirée Artôt. He spent most of his time in her company,

Désirée Artôt, the Belgian mezzo-soprano to whom Tchaikovsky was briefly engaged

composed music for her, wrote enthusiastic letters about her to his family, indeed showed every sign of obsession. 'Artôt is a wonderful person,' he wrote to his sister, 'and we have become the very closest of friends. I'm busy now writing recitatives and choruses for Auber's *Domino noir*, which must be done in time for her benefit performance.' Later, he apologised to his brother Anatoly for having been out of touch, 'but circumstances have played havoc with my correspondence. The fact is, I've been devoting every minute of my spare time to a person I suspect you may have heard of, and for whom I feel great affection.' By this time the gossip had got around that she and Tchaikovsky were engaged to be married. On the 26 December 1868, he wrote to his father:

> *I suspect that rumours may have reached you of my engagement, and that you may have taken umbrage at my not having written to you on the subject. Let me explain without further ado. I first met Artôt in the spring, but only at a supper party after her benefit performance. I didn't see her again until a month after her return here in the autumn, when we chanced to meet at a musical soirée. She expressed surprise at my neglect, after which I promised to visit her, but I wouldn't have kept the promise (you know how hard I find getting to know people) if Anton Rubinstein hadn't almost dragged me to her house. From then on she fairly showered me with daily invitations and I became accustomed to calling on her every evening. It wasn't long before we became inflamed with feelings of great affection for one another, resulting at once in a mutual understanding (you know what I mean). Needless to say, there soon arose the question of marriage, which we both desire and hope to accomplish this summer, if nothing happens to prevent it.*

In fact, circumstances, people and forces beyond Tchaikovsky's control were at that very moment conspiring to prevent it. Nikolay Rubinstein and other friends were appalled at the idea, and made no secret of it.

> *They say that in marrying a famous singer I shall be cast in the pathetic role of being my wife's husband – that I shall traipse along behind her all over Europe, living off her income and finding work impossible. They warn that when my ardour has cooled, I shall find my self-esteem lost in a maelstrom of disillusionment and despair. This, of course, could be avoided if she were to settle down to a domestic life with me in Russia, but in spite of all her love for me, she cannot contemplate abandoning the stage, to which she has become accustomed and which has brought her fame and money in equal measure. But I love her with all my heart and soul, and cannot bear any longer to live without her. Yet common sense urges me to draw back, before it's too late.*

In the event, the matter was decided, in the most unexpected manner, by the lady herself. Tchaikovsky's response, in a letter to Modest, is significant beyond its brevity.

> *The Artôt business has resolved itself in the most amusing way. In Warsaw she has fallen in love with the baritone Padilla – the object of her scorn when she was here – and she is marrying him! But you would need to know the details of our relationship to have any notion of how funny this dénouement is.*

The details were not forthcoming, but it seemed clear to Modest, as to all who knew Tchaikovsky well, that his amusement was genuine – indeed that it masked (very thinly) an unspoken sense of relief. It was certainly the last time he found anything to laugh at in his relations with women.

For the moment, in any case, he had other things to think about. High on the list was his imminent professional debut as a conductor, in his own *Characteristic Dances*. But as his friend Nikolay Kashkin recalled, there was nothing to suggest a great career in the making:

> *I went backstage, and he told me that, to his own surprise, he was not feeling in the least apprehensive. We talked briefly, after which I went off to my seat in the hall. Soon afterwards Pyotr Il'yich appeared, and it was obvious at a glance that he had gone completely to pieces. The orchestral players were already arranged on stage, and he walked between their desks bending forward, as though desiring to hide himself. By the time he reached the podium he had the look of a desperate man. He totally forgot his own piece – unable, apparently, to see anything in the score – and failed to give the players their most essential cues. Fortunately they knew the piece well and were able to disregard his hopeless directions. Indeed they managed quite a creditable performance, merely smiling when they looked towards the composer.*

It was at around this time that Tchaikovsky first met Hector Berlioz, whose music had – and was still having – a formative influence on his own, particularly with regard to orchestration. Berlioz was in Moscow to conduct concerts of his own music, and Tchaikovsky was able to witness for the first time a truly great composer-conductor, the greatest, indeed, of his time. Until the rise of Wagner, Berlioz had no rivals.

Although Berlioz's visit marked a turning point in Tchaikovsky's career as a composer, Berlioz himself, ironically, had little to do with it. It was due to his concerts, however, and for this reason alone, that Mily Balakirev, the lynchpin of the nationalist movement in Russian music, left his stronghold in St Petersburg and came to Moscow. Balakirev was the dominant force in a group of five composers – the others being Mussorgsky, Borodin, Rimsky-Korsakov and Cui – known collectively as the 'Mighty Handful'. (In elaborating this metaphor, it must be said that César Cui, a lifelong critic of Tchaikovsky's music, was decidedly the little finger, for if there was anything mighty about him at all it was restricted to his sense of self-importance and the abandon with which he wielded his critical pen.)

These five composers, all amateurs, and essentially self-taught, bewailed the centuries-old domination of Russian culture by imported western-European styles and values, the principal legacy of Peter the Great. Like Mikhail Glinka, who started the movement in the first half of the century, they espoused a music founded on the styles and principles of indigenous Russian folk music, regarding western-influenced, conservatoire-trained musicians like Tchaikovsky and the Rubinsteins with deep suspicion, if not indeed as traitors to their birthright. At the time of Balakirev's visit to Moscow, however, Tchaikovsky was still young enough to be influenced – to be 'saved' – and Balakirev, self-anointed, took on the role of saviour.

To read the correspondence between them is to marvel at Tchaikovsky's docility in the face of Balakirev's overweening self-confidence. Balakirev was the only man who ever persuaded Tchaikovsky to rewrite a work several times over. The reason he succeeded is not simply because he was forceful to the point of brutality, but because he was so often right, and Tchaikovsky knew it. He could never match Tchaikovsky in genius or sophistication, and never pretended otherwise; but he had a powerful native intelligence, an instinctive but finely honed understanding of musical language, and a kind

Balakirev was the only man who persuaded Tchaikovsky to rewrite a work, because he was right, and Tchaikovsky knew it.

of raw insight into dramatic psychology for which many opera composers would have given their eye teeth (though apart from admiring Glinka he had no interest in opera himself). It is a demonstrable fact that it was largely due to Balakirev's bullying that the fantasy overture **Romeo and Juliet** of 1870 turned out to be Tchaikovsky's first authentic masterpiece. Ironically, under the circumstances, it was also the first piece in which his own musical personality was evident from first note to last, and in which he unfurled the most beautiful theme he had yet composed. Subsequently known as the 'love theme', it even became the basis of an American popular song in the 1930s.

It would be wrong to believe that Tchaikovsky's interest

Mily Alexeyevich Balakirev (de facto leader of the 'Mighty Handful'), whose forceful persuasion resulted in Tchaikovsky producing his first orchestral masterpiece, Romeo and Juliet

in Russian folk music, or indeed his attraction to musical nationalism, dated from his acquaintance with Balakirev. Since his teens (when he composed **Zemfira's Song**), he had been writing music just as Russian in style, content and spirit as anything by the 'Mighty Handful'. A case in point is his opera *Voyevoda* ('The Provincial Governor') of 1868, followed by the arrangement for piano duet of fifty Russian folksongs. And his next three operas followed suit.

In November 1874, having overcome his earlier generic aversion, he started work on his **First Piano Concerto**. Early in 1875 he played it over to Nikolay Rubinstein. To Tchaikovsky's distressed bemusement, this most dedicated of champions pronounced the work unplayable and tore into it with a ferocity that left the composer literally trembling.

> *I might as well have been a madman, some incompetent, ignorant hack who had had the unpardonable effrontery to pester the famous musician with my cheap trash! And to think that such a merciless harangue should be inflicted on one who had already composed a great deal and who taught the free composition course at the Conservatoire. I left the room abruptly, without a word, and went upstairs. My fury and consternation were such that I could barely speak. Rubinstein soon appeared and, observing my obvious distress, called me into another room, where he simply repeated that the concerto was impossible and, after citing numerous passages requiring what amounted to recomposition, let fall that if I acceded to his demands, and to a timetable set by himself, he would do me the honour of playing the work in one of his concerts. 'I refuse to change a single note', I replied. 'I will publish it exactly as it stands today!' And I did.*

Hans von Bülow, who gave the first performance of Tchaikovsky's Piano Concerto No. 1

The work had its premiere (without Rubinstein, of course) not in Russia but in Boston, Massachusetts, with the great German pianist-conductor Hans von Bülow (son-in-law of Franz Liszt and one of the legendary pianists of the century) as soloist. Rubinstein – who later recanted and became one of the work's foremost champions – was thus thoroughly upstaged.

All in all, 1875 had been a good year for Tchaikovsky, and it was crowned by the joy of a new friendship, with the French composer and pianist Camille Saint-Saëns, who was visiting Moscow on a concert tour. Different though the two men were, Tchaikovsky was immediately well disposed to Saint-Saëns and genuinely admired his music, noting that it combined 'the grace and charm of the French school with the depth and earnestness of the great German masters.' He was also enchanted by Saint-Saëns' wit, and in awe, alike, of his comprehensive musicianship, his originality as a thinker, his formidable breadth of knowledge, and his astonishing record of achievement. In addition to his mastery of composition, Saint-Saëns was a first-rate pianist, an unsurpassed sight-reader and score-reader, an accomplished conductor, and in Liszt's view 'the greatest organist in the world.' He was also a published poet, a playwright, an amateur astronomer (a member of the French Astronomical Society and a contributor to scientific journals), an

1875 had been a good year for Tchaikovsky, crowned by the joy of a new friendship with Camille Saint-Saëns.

influential critic, one of the first true musicologists, and, as one might expect, a man of supreme self-confidence. Berlioz said of him, 'Saint-Saëns knows everything; but he lacks inexperience.'

The initial friendship of these dissimilar brothers-in-art resulted in one of the most bizarre, star-studded and ill-attended productions in theatrical history. Among their soon-discovered bonds was a great fondness not only for ballet but, perhaps more significantly, for impersonating female dancers. As Modest relates:

> *This suggested the idea of their dancing together, and they brought out a little ballet,* Pygmalion and Galatea, *on the stage of the Conservatoire. Saint-Saëns, aged forty, played the part of Galatea, most conscientiously, while Tchaikovsky, aged thirty-five, appeared as Pygmalion. Nikolay Rubinstein formed the orchestra. Unfortunately, besides the three performers, there were no spectators to witness this singular entertainment.*

Also unfortunately, Tchaikovsky's hopes that their friendship would prove an asset in his professional future came to naught. Long afterwards, Modest tells us, they met again, as comparative strangers, and remained so thereafter.

Far more significant was the influence of another French composer whom Tchaikovsky came across, albeit posthumously, only weeks after his pas de deux with Saint-Saëns. In December 1876 Tchaikovsky and Modest visited Paris, where they attended a performance of Bizet's opera *Carmen*, which neither had heard before. Tchaikovsky at once conceived what Modest deemed a 'quite unhealthy passion' for the music, and it would be only a slight exaggeration to say that his own music was never the same again. Tchaikovsky became obsessed with the fate-laden atmosphere

In December 1876 Tchaikovsky attended a performance of Bizet's opera *Carmen*, and at once conceived a 'quite unhealthy passion' for the music.

and the sheer raw emotionalism of the work, characteristics which now began entering his own music to a higher degree than ever before. For his next opera, and under the direct influence of *Carmen*, he thought of adapting the Fifth Canto of Dante's *Inferno*, dealing with the story of Francesca da Rimini. For various reasons, one being problems with the libretto, he opted in the end for an orchestral rather than an operatic work; but the result was dramatic enough for any theatre – in fact considerably more dramatic than his next and most famous opera was to be.

For his next opera, under the direct influence of *Carmen*, he thought of adapting the Fifth Canto of Dante's *Inferno*.

Commentators and biographers have often cited the extreme emotionalism of *Francesca da Rimini* as evidence of Tchaikovsky's frame of mind. Yet from exactly the same period comes his lightweight almost demure **Variations on a Rococo Theme** for cello and orchestra. Few works composed at the same time by the same composer have ever been more strikingly different than these.

The idea that one can deduce a composer's state of mind from the works that he or she writes at any given moment is easy enough to accept when you have a composer as blatantly emotional as Tchaikovsky, but the truth is necessarily more subtle and more complicated. No artist, in any medium, can afford (or manage) to experience the emotion being expressed while in the act of depicting it. Nor, of course, is it even necessary to have had certain emotional experiences in order to represent them in a way that rings true to the audience, who in all likelihood will never have had them either. In order to depict a murderer or a heartless libertine with searing and haunting immediacy, it is not necessary to have been either. Nor might it be an asset. The essential requirements are a vivid imagination, exceptional psychological insight and a consummate mastery of the art in question.

All art is symbolic. Nowhere is this more succinctly or

delightfully demonstrated than in René Magritte's painting of a pipe, with its painted, parenthetical statement: 'This is not a pipe'. Almost as pithy is a story about Picasso, who was asked by a stranger why he didn't paint people the way they really are. 'What exactly do you mean?' he replied. 'Well, for instance,' said the man, producing a photo from his wallet, 'this is my wife.' 'Oh, I see,' said Picasso, 'but isn't she awfully small and flat?'

In the difference between *Francesca da Rimini* and the *Variations on a Rococo Theme* lies what may well be the most important key for unlocking the secrets of Tchaikovsky's inner life: namely the almost continual struggle between despair and hope, between the passionate chaos of his emotional intensity and the carefully structured ordering of its articulation through music. It is not unreasonable to suspect that at least a part of his reverence for Mozart was a longing for the clear-cut ideals and assumptions of the late eighteenth century: the dedication to proportion, symmetry and restraint, the channelling of emotion into preordained forms. Mozart, whose works Tchaikovsky knew better than most people did (certainly in Russia), was perhaps the most Utopian of all composers. In the majority of his output, certainly the piano concertos and most of the operas, the opposing tensions which provide the main engine for musical, dramatic and psychological movement are almost always finally resolved. Even the turbulent D minor Piano Concerto, the one most beloved by the nineteenth-century Romantics, ends in sunshine. But Tchaikovsky was never cut out to be a Utopian. In their sharing of sorrows, their unashamed confession of confused and tormented emotions, his greatest works – *Eugene Onegin*, the last three symphonies, *Manfred*, for instance – may console, include, even entertain the listener, but they are seldom guilty of optimism even if some of them aim rather strenuously in that direction. It would be wrong, however, to tag Tchaikovsky as a tragedian. His emotional scope (unlike that of Mozart, Beethoven and Shakespeare) was not all-embracing, but it ranged wide and was explored with exceptional variety and colour. Among his many other virtues he was a born entertainer with a keen sense of theatre, reflected as much in his purely orchestral music as in his works for the stage.

Interlude II: Tchaikovsky in the Theatre

From an early age, Tchaikovsky was attracted to the theatre as a moth is to a flame. His attraction to ballet in particular was no surprise. Dance was not only a vital part of Russia's cultural tradition, but an essential ingredient in Tchaikovsky's artistic bloodstream. It played a prominent part in his earliest repertoire; at the age of nine, he delighted in accompanying family and friends at the piano while they danced. The element of dance, both formal and embedded, became a prominent part of his compositional output, basically from start to finish (ending with the waltz in 5/4 time in his last symphony). He was also fascinated and moved by the expressive power of human movement, especially in women. Among the first of the qualities he extolled to Modest in describing Désirée Artôt were 'the eloquence of her gestures and the grace of her movements and poses', and he made something of a fetish of impersonating female dancers. His pre-eminence as a ballet composer was therefore almost predictable, the only major surprise being the relative lateness of its arrival.

Dance was an essential ingredient in Tchaikovsky's artistic bloodstream.

Also formative, though not perhaps so deeply ingrained in his psyche, was his early experience of opera, or the music therefrom – in the theatre, in the home (courtesy of the family's orchestrion) and in the concert hall. Defending his theatrical work to a sceptic, he declared that 'to refrain from writing operas is the act of a hero, and we have only one such hero in our time – Johannes Brahms. Heroism of that kind is not for me. The stage, with all its glitter, lures me irresistibly.' But there was more to it than mere glitter and attraction. Opera had practical advantages of which he was well aware when he wrote:

> *The stage often paralyses a composer's musical inspiration, with the result that symphonic and chamber music stand, in general, far higher than operatic music. A symphony or a sonata imposes no limitations on me; opera, on the other hand, possesses a different advantage: it grants us the possibility to speak in the musical language of the people, and more frequently, too. An opera may be given forty times in a single season, a symphony maybe once in a decade.*

Tchaikovsky's first opera, in its overtly nationalist flavour, set the tone for the next three. (Thereafter, even when dealing with Russian subjects, his approach was to be more cosmopolitan.) Completed in 1868, *Voyevoda* was a folk opera (like Glinka's *Ruslan and Lyudmila*, which had been the first of its kind, and influential to an epoch-making degree). *Voyevoda* began as a collaboration with his considerably older friend, the playwright Alexander Ostrovsky, to be based on his drama of the same name, but ended up with a libretto by Tchaikovsky himself. It contained some excellent music and is as lavishly folkish as anything he wrote. It also set the pattern of many Tchaikovsky premieres in being liked by the public but condemned by the critics. In the words of one such, it was 'completely lacking in any Russian quality, indeed in any Russian national element at all.' This, while preposterous and inaccurate, was predictably discouraging to Tchaikovsky, who destroyed

Voyevoda set the pattern of many Tchaikovsky premieres in being liked by the public but condemned by the critics.

the score – though not before salvaging the best of it, much of which he later recycled. He was never one to abandon favourite progeny.

His next two attempts (*Undine* and *Mandragora*, both from 1869) foundered before they were completed. *The Oprichnik*, composed in 1872, is therefore the first wholly extant Tchaikovsky opera, but it is significant for more than that reason alone. It also gives us inspiring evidence of Tchaikovsky's sheer tenacity when it came to what he believed was genuinely good: much of its best music, though set to different words and applied to different situations, is lifted more or less wholesale from *Voyevoda*, and in one instance Tchaikovsky also imports music from his failed symphonic fantasia *Fatum* of 1868. Interesting, too, is the way he approaches theatrical 'realism' in the treatment of a historical subject (the Oprichniks were the bodyguards of Ivan the Terrible), especially in the light of two recent examples of broadly similar dramas – Rimsky-Korsakov's *The Maid of Pskov*, which also deals with Ivan the Terrible, and Mussorgsky's *Boris Godunov* (which Tchaikovsky intensely disliked). *The Oprichnik* may be Russian in subject and also in much of its music, but in treatment it stands more closely to the grand operas of Meyerbeer, associated with the Paris Opéra of the 1830s and '40s. There is an element of gaudy sensationalism that he was eventually to abandon. Ironically, *The Oprichnik* was his first operatic success in terms of the box office, the irony arising from his own very considerable dissatisfaction with it. Had he not already parted with the rights, he would have prevented the opera's revivals.

The Oprichnik was his first operatic success in terms of the box office, the irony arising from his own very considerable dissatisfaction with it.

With *Vakula the Smith* (1874), a return to folk opera, he finally produced an opera he felt happy with, despite the fact that much of its music sounds more like Balakirev. For this work, the usual pattern of reception was reversed: the critics (even the normally hostile César Cui) liked it, but the public remained largely indifferent. Even its revision nine years later as *Cherevichki* ('The Little Slippers') failed to improve its fortunes much, yet the music, while redolent of Glinka and Bellini, is full of delights. It is hard to understand the almost total neglect of the work today, though there is at least a fine recording of it.

CD 1
track 12
www.naxosbooks.com

Neglect is something that Tchaikovsky's next opera has never known. **Eugene Onegin**, though arising out of the most agonised period of his life (see Chapter 4), is a perennial favourite all over the world. Based on Alexander Pushkin's verse novel of the same name, it is rightly described (on its title page) not as an opera, precisely, but as 'Lyrical or Elegiac Scenes in Three Acts'. It gives us the very essence of Tchaikovsky at his best, and was written with an ease and speed all the more surprising in the circumstances. A story of unrequited love, cynical manipulation, tragedy and rejection, it parallels in many respects the events, misunderstandings and mixed motives of Tchaikovsky's own life at the time. Yet it is leavened with infectious (if ironic) gaiety, pastoral poetry, the highlife (and lowlife) of both town and country, and, above all, a sustained level of lyrical beauty and psychological insight unique in his music up to that point. Unusually for Tchaikovsky, the emotion, while neither prettified nor constrained, is expressed without a hint of exaggeration (let alone hysteria), and the drama derives more from character than action. He himself recognised that the minimal stagecraft required might lessen its appeal to audiences reared on spectacle, but his misgivings proved unfounded. It is significant that while composing what is essentially a tragedy, he was in deep personal crisis yet was able to write: 'Criticise *Onegin* if you wish, but I am composing the music with

Eugene Onegin, based on Alexander Pushkin's verse novel of the same name, gives us the very essence of Tchaikovsky at his best.

tremendous enjoyment.' And there's the miracle. In this most Mozartian of all his operas, Tchaikovsky succeeds in wringing our withers while leaving us with a profound sense of satisfaction and poetic fulfilment. There have been plenty in every generation who have taken him up on his offer and criticised *Onegin*. No one, including the composer, has ever claimed it to be a perfect work, but it is a magical one, and it works its magic with a strange, unexpected and peculiarly congruous charm, despite the darkness of the story.

No one, including the composer, has ever claimed *Onegin* to be a perfect work, but it is a magical one.

Writing *Onegin* was obviously cathartic for Tchaikovsky, and it was perhaps in hopes of a repeat release that he turned almost at once, as a follow-up, to the subject of Joan of Arc. There is certainly something manic in his declaration at the time that 'The idea of the *Maid of Orleans* has taken furious possession of me. I want to finish the whole work in an hour, as sometimes happens in a dream.' It took a little longer, but perhaps not long enough. The result was a hit-and-miss affair on an epic scale. His clear subjective identification with Joan produced the best music, as had his identification with Tatiana in *Onegin*, and there are many good things elsewhere. But Tchaikovsky is back in Meyerbeer mode. He has lost that sense of self that did the trick in *Onegin*; indeed he seems often to be attempting to escape from himself (quite understandably in view of his troubles at the time). Almost everything is reduced to the level of a rather pretentious costume ball, with characterisation supplanted by caricature, drama by melodrama, psychology by action. It failed in Russia, but with a kind of tragic irony became the first Tchaikovsky opera to be produced abroad – where it also failed.

With his next two operas, *Mazeppa* (1881–3) and *The Sorceress* (1885–7), his operatic slump continued. Tchaikovsky was never primarily a dramatist with a flair for the epic canvas (as was Tolstoy). He was not a searing, powerful realist like Mussorgsky. He lacked Verdi's genius for characterisation irrespective of subjective identification; and the world of Wagnerian music drama, though Tchaikovsky was certainly influenced by it, was far from his natural home. He produced his best only when he could 'inhabit' his characters, as he could and did with both the leads in *Onegin*. Why, then, did he choose to attempt *Mazeppa* or *The Sorceress*, in which sympathetic characters are in depressingly short supply?

Whatever the intermittent virtues of his other stage works composed by this time, *Onegin* stood alone in terms of overall quality and vision. In no other opera had he emerged as a truly major player on the world stage, least of all in the three composed in its wake. However, with **The Queen of Spades** (1890), also known as *Pique Dame*, it had company. A fascinating tale of love and gambling, again adapted from Pushkin, it is this work rather than *Onegin* that in the view of many marks the summit of Tchaikovsky's achievement as an opera composer, particularly in Russia. While the line between drama and melodrama remains fine, and is occasionally crossed, even the melodrama is brought off supremely well, and the characterisation is of a generally high order throughout. As in *Onegin* the drama is character-based rather than action-based, and the score contains some of his best and most exciting music. As a composer, and as a man, Tchaikovsky's heart was essentially lyrical rather than heroic. This is not to say, however, that he lacked either passion or drama. Far from it: he was liberally endowed with both. In *The Queen of Spades*, perhaps more than in any of his other operas, he was truest to his heart in the widest possible way.

CD 1
track 10
www.naxosbooks.com

The Queen of Spades in the view of many marks the summit of Tchaikovsky's achievement as an opera composer, particularly in Russia.

It would have been satisfying if his operatic career had ended on a high like that. Sadly, it ended with a curious, overblown one-acter called *Iolanta* (not to be confused with Gilbert and Sullivan's *Iolanthe*, though often transliterated to read that way). This rather depressing little drama – the choice of subject was Tchaikovsky's own – is about a blind, fifteenth-century princess, blackmailed into undergoing a sight-giving operation despite having no idea of what sight is, or of the difference between herself and other people. In fact she has no desire for sight. It was commissioned to balance the two-act *Nutcracker* ballet, but the two works were only once produced as such. Though redeemed by pretty, even touching music, *Iolanta* finds Tchaikovsky way under par and providing a pale reflection, almost a caricature, of his finer self.

Onegin and *The Queen of Spades* notwithstanding, the most enduringly popular of all Tchaikovsky's stage works are to be found not among his operas but in the three great ballets: *Swan Lake* (1876), *The Sleeping Beauty* (1889) and *The Nutcracker* (1892). Indeed it might fairly be claimed that these remain the three most famous and familiar ballets of all time, repeatedly performed on stage and screen alike. Apart from the entrancing music, rich in melody, orchestral colour and rhythmic variety, they redefined the nature of ballet music in Russia.

The most enduringly popular of all Tchaikovsky's stage works are to be found not among his operas but in the three great ballets: *Swan Lake, The Sleeping Beauty* and *The Nutcracker.*

Swan Lake, which quite rapidly became one of the most popular works ever written, was not at first well received. And to pile irony on irony, it failed, in large part, not because the critics judged the music to be inadequate but because they thought it was too good. Up to that time, ballet music in Russia (unlike in France) was regarded as little more than a convenient and generally pleasant background to the dancing on stage – which, of course, is what the audience had come to see. The standard fare was provided by such relatively undistinguished composers as Minkus, Gerber, Pugni and Adam. (How many people today could whistle a single tune by any of them?) The function of ballet music was to be suitably atmospheric, but discreet. The music should on no account be distracting, and above all it should not indulge in the vivid characterisation which is the lifeblood of opera. Tchaikovsky, however, was never cut out to accompany puppets, and *Swan Lake* was considered too operatic by half.

From early childhood, as we have seen, Tchaikovsky's relation to music was overwhelmingly, perhaps uniquely, emotional. He could no more distance himself from his characters than he could get up on the stage and dance the roles himself. He moved the goal posts, as it were. The reason he could get away with it, as he eventually did, was because he had a genius for melody, melody that cried out to be danced to. His sense of theatrical atmosphere was second to none, and he could paint with an orchestra better than even the greatest set-designers of the time could paint the scenery. Here, although his contributions were frustratingly few, Tchaikovsky was in his element.

Chapter 3

Celebrity and Crisis 1876–1877

Celebrity and Crisis 1876–1877

The emotional floodgates opened in Tchaikovsky by Bizet's *Carmen* affected far more than his music. They served to intensify the inner turmoil occasioned by his still largely secret sexuality. In Russia as elsewhere at that time homosexuality was generally regarded as a disease, which was at least potentially 'curable'. It was far commoner than generally acknowledged but was still very much 'the Love that dare not speak its name' (to use Lord Alfred Douglas's famous phrase). In the highly confused and ambivalent hope of resolving his difficulties in this line, Tchaikovsky made the most misguided, indeed calamitous, decision of his life. In September 1876 he wrote to Modest, who was also homosexual:

> *I am now going through a very critical period of my life. I won't go into detail now, but will simply tell you that* I have decided to marry. *It is unavoidable. Something that I have to do – not only for myself but for you, Modest, as well, and for Tolya, and Sasha, indeed for all those whom I love. During this period my vision of myself has changed significantly, with the result that from this time forward I will make serious preparations for matrimony – regardless of the identity of the other party. I now firmly believe that for both of us (you*

and I), our dispositions are the greatest and most insoluble impediment to our happiness and that we must fight our natures with all our strength.

For all the evident firmness of its resolve, this letter suggests a certain confusion, even ambivalence. If one truly believes an obstacle to be insuperable, then fighting it, let alone with all one's strength, is a futile waste of vital resources. But nothing reveals Tchaikovsky's panic more alarmingly than his determination to prepare for marriage 'regardless of the identity of the other party'. Her identity was the least of it, for there was no other party.

More real, but likewise unidentified, is the nature of the insuperable obstacle itself. The true crisis for Tchaikovsky is not his own 'nature' but society's attitude to it. The idea that he was tormented with guilt over his sexual orientation and that it was this that ultimately precipitated his death is a demonstrable fiction. The real reason for his shock decision is strongly implied in a single sentence, also addressed to Modest: 'I will do everything in my power to get married *this* year – and if I lack the necessary courage, I will at any rate abandon my habits *forever* and will try to stop people regarding me as "one of the old dears".' One of the abiding conflicts of Tchaikovsky's inner life was between his perception of himself and his chronic hunger for the approbation of others – the conflict between his burning integrity and his tormenting self-doubt. His evident ambivalence about 'the old dears' arose, again, not from their homosexuality per se but from their own attitudes to it, and their consequent behaviour. Also significant in this revealing sentence is his use of the word 'habits' – now distancing his behaviour from his 'nature' and equating it, implicitly, with his smoking, drinking and reckless spending.

The idea that he was tormented with guilt over his sexual orientation is a demonstrable fiction.

Modest was sceptical about his brother's plans, to say the least, and deeply anxious as to their origin. He encouraged him, in vain, to disregard whatever people might say or think about his inclinations. Tchaikovsky himself took a subtler and predictably more complex view:

> *I understand what you say, but only up to a point. There are those who cannot be contemptuous of my vices simply because they came to love me before suspecting that my reputation is, in fact, already ruined . . . Surely you must understand how it hurts me to know that people 'pity' and 'forgive' me when the truth is, I am guilty of nothing! How deeply distressing it is to realise that those who love me are sometimes also ashamed of me! This has happened time and again already and, of course, will happen countless more times. To put it bluntly, I seek marriage, or some sort of public relationship with a woman, so as to silence various despicable creatures whose opinions I value not at all, but who are in a position to cause distress to those near to me.*

Here he presents his decision as based entirely on altruism. Perhaps the most significant line in this letter, however, is the sentence: 'There are those who cannot be contemptuous of my vices simply because they came to love me *before* suspecting that my reputation is, in fact, already ruined.' He speaks not of himself at all but only of his reputation. Nevertheless, however rationally and selflessly he may have thought he was approaching the matter, it was taking a terrible toll on his peace of mind. On his way back from a trip to Germany, he confided:

> *I arrived at Verbovka in an appalling mental state, my nerves completely shattered. A couple of weeks ago there*

> *were reasons enough for my spirits to rise a little, but the fact is that there are hours, days, weeks, and months when everything seems black, when you are certain that nobody cares for you, that you have been jettisoned, abandoned by one and all. Apart from the fact that my nerves have always been weak and sensitive, my depression derives precisely from my bachelor state,* from the absence in my life of any element of self-sacrifice *[author's emphasis]. To my vocation, yes, I do live up to that, to the best of my abilities, but the fact is I am utterly useless to anyone. If I were to vanish from the face of the earth today, then Russian music might suffer some small loss, but it would be no more than that.*

It was at this very point, as though on cue from some capricious fate, that two women entered Tchaikovsky's life. They were soon to occupy a central part in it. One was mature, highly cultured and unimaginably wealthy; the other was young, unsophisticated, not evidently very bright, and far from rich.

Nadezhda Filaretovna von Meck was the forty-four-year-old widow of a hugely prosperous railway baron. Of their eighteen children, eleven survived and seven still lived with her. When she travelled, as she frequently did, it was on her own special trains, with her family and domestic household in attendance, these always including a hired musician to play for her. One of these, in later years, was the young Debussy. In 1876, however, this position was occupied by a former pupil and close friend of Tchaikovsky's, the violinist Yosif Kotek. Since the death of her husband, Mme von Meck had become a recluse who avowedly abhorred humanity at large. For the most part, her contact with the outside world was limited to the reports of a close circle of informants, one of whom was Nikolay Rubinstein.

Mme von Meck began to send him large sums of money, but on one very strange condition: they should never meet. And they never did.

It was through Kotek and Rubinstein that she became acquainted with Tchaikovsky's music. After a few generous commissions of mostly minor works and arrangements, she entered into a long and often complex correspondence with Tchaikovsky, the like of which has never been seen before or since. She also began to send him large sums of money, but on one very strange condition: they should never meet. And they never did. On two occasions, they did actually see one another, but passed by without a word. Yet under these bizarre circumstances they developed, through music and correspondence alone, the most intimate and passionate friendship either of them had ever known. Putting her own cards on the table at the outset, Mme von Meck expressed herself in unique terms and provided Tchaikovsky with a verbal self-portrait whose unguarded intimacy and fearless candour seized, and held, his attention:

Nadezhda von Meck, who supported Tchaikovsky financially and emotionally for many years

Being entirely devoid of femininity, I am unsympathetic in all of my personal relations. Tenderness is quite alien to my character, a trait passed on to my entire family, all of whom have a horror of affectation and sentimentality. Our relationships are thus comradely, even masculine, one might say, rather than being in any way intimate.

She may have been afraid of sentimentality, but she was hardly afraid of expressing emotion. Well before the annuity that effectively made Tchaikovsky a rich man, she wrote to him in terms that would normally have frightened and offended him:

As soon as I felt the impact of your music, I felt I had to find out as much as possible about the man who wrote it. I began to seek out every scrap of information about you, seizing every chance to hear something, canvassing public opinion, reading and listening to individual judgments, alerting myself to every passing remark. And I found that very often what others most criticised in you would lead me *to* ecstasy. *I want to discover everything there is to know about you, so that I can know at almost any time just where you are and even what you may be doing. From everything I have observed in you and have heard from other sources, both pro and con, I have conceived the kindest, most cordial and enthusiastic feelings for you.*

Given the tone of these opening salvos, it comes as no surprise that kindliness, cordiality and enthusiasm soon gave way to something infinitely more intense. With almost every letter, Mme von Meck came less and less to resemble the self-portrait offered at the start of their correspondence:

There is no one else in the world who affords me such deep and sublime happiness as you do. I am grateful for this beyond words, and can only pray that this joyousness never ends, never changes, for such a thing would devastate me. I cannot describe the effect on me of your dear letters, or convey to you what balm they are to my wearied heart, possessed by such uncontrollable longing. When I enter my sitting room and spy on the table an envelope bearing your dear, familiar handwriting, it is like a whiff of ether that puts an end to all pain. The love I bear you is also fate, which my will is powerless to resist. When I hear your music, I surrender to you utterly; you are deified for me. Everything that is most pure, most generous, most sublime rises up in me, from the very depth of my soul!

This sounds uncommonly like the early stages of a love affair. Tchaikovsky, albeit a little later, responds in kind: 'I love you with all the strength of my soul. Every minute I bless the fate that brought you into my life. With each new letter I wonder afresh at your astonishing kindness.'

Though nothing overtly sexual ever creeps into their correspondence, the more one reads, the harder it is to believe that there was not a strong psychosexual element on both sides. If there had been a woman composer who wrote music just like Tchaikovsky's, it seems improbable that Mme von Meck would have undertaken the correspondence in the first place. Furthermore, there is an unmistakable element of jealousy in her references to the second woman who dominated Tchaikovsky's life in the early part of their correspondence.

In the spring of 1877, quite out of the blue, Tchaikovsky received a letter (which he appears to have destroyed) from a clearly infatuated girl, one Antonina Milyukova, who claimed to have been in his class at the Conservatoire. Tchaikovsky himself had no memory of her, and was in any case already accustomed to getting letters of this kind. However, this one differed from all its predecessors and lodged itself in Tchaikovsky's mind at once, where it stubbornly remained. As he reported to Mme von Meck: 'I learned from her letter that she had loved me for some time. It was written so genuinely, and with such warmth, that I decided to answer it – something I had avoided in similar cases before. And although I offered her no hope of reciprocity, there sprang up a correspondence between us.'

Quite out of the blue, Tchaikovsky received a letter from a clearly infatuated girl, who claimed to have been in his class at the Conservatoire.

Notwithstanding Mme von Meck's ignorance, at this point, of Tchaikovsky's marital project, his bulletins on this new woman in his life can hardly have been a welcome development. 'She is twenty-eight years old,' he later reported, 'and actually quite pretty. She has a spotless reputation, and out of love of independence she has been living for some time on her own earnings, although she has a very loving mother. She is virtually penniless, not highly educated, self-evidently kind, and would seem to be quite capable of forming permanent relationships.' If this last line struck a chill into Mme von Meck's heart, she never confessed it.

Although Tchaikovsky claimed to have no memory of Milyukova, her account of their earlier acquaintance suggests either that Tchaikovsky was lying (which is improbable) or that she was already deeply mired in a fantasy world of her own (which, in the light of future events, is a near certainty). As she recollected many years later, she had enrolled at the Conservatoire in the early 1870s and was:

> *... blissfully happy there, meeting him constantly; he was always very affectionate towards me. For four years and more I had loved him in secret. I knew perfectly well that he liked me, but he was shy, and I knew he would never have made a proposal himself. I pledged myself to go to the chapel at the Spassky Gates every day for six weeks to pray for him, no matter what the weather. When the six weeks were up, I ordered a liturgy in the chapel and, following further prayer at home, I decided to post him a letter in which I poured out to him on paper all the love that had gathered in my heart over so many years. He answered me at once, and we began to correspond.*

Of that correspondence, none of Tchaikovsky's letters have survived, and the first extant letter from her to him is probably her third:

> *I see that I must already begin to restrain my feelings, which you yourself indicated to me in your first letter. Now, even*

though I can't see you, I am comforted by the thought that you are in the same city with me, whereas in a month, or perhaps even less, you will most likely leave, and God knows if we shall ever see one another again, since I, too, plan to leave Moscow. But wherever I may be, I will never be able to forget you and will never stop loving you. After you, I never want even to look at another man.

In fact, Tchaikovsky had already left Moscow. On discovering this, Antonina immediately wrote again, her tone now changed:

Could you really end our correspondence without seeing me even once? I am certain you could not be so cruel! My love for you only doubled after reading your last letter – and your shortcomings are of no matter to me. Had you been perfect, I might have remained quite cool toward you. But now I am dying with longing, burning with a desire to see you. No 'flaw' in your character could ever make me stop loving you. This is not a momentary infatuation, but a feeling that has grown in me over a very long time. I am now quite unable to extinguish it, nor have I any wish to. All I can think of is the moment when I see you again. I shall be ready to throw my arms around your neck and smother you with kisses. My first ever kiss will be given to you and to no one else in the world.

So far, so predictable, if hardly desirable. But as she closes, she changes the game:

Farewell, my dearest. Do not attempt to disappoint me further. You would only be wasting your time. For I cannot live without you, which is why soon, perhaps, I shall have to

kill myself. So let me look at you, and kiss you, so that the memory of that kiss will remain with me in the next world.
Farewell.
Eternally yours,
A.M.

Not wanting a suicide on his conscience, Tchaikovsky agreed to see her on his return to Moscow, and instantly regretted it:

Why ever did I do this? It's almost as though some power of fate was drawing me towards her. When I saw her I very clearly reiterated that the only feelings I had for her were of sympathy and of gratitude for her love. But afterwards, I wondered about it – reflecting on the frivolity of my action. If I really neither loved her nor wanted to give her any encouragement, why, then, had I visited her; and what would it lead to? I realised after her next letter that if I suddenly turned away from her, having already gone this far, I would shatter her happiness, very possibly bringing her to a tragic end. So, one fine evening, I visited her once more, and told her frankly, yet again, that I did not love her but that I would at least be her devoted and grateful friend. I warned her that I am an irritable, unpredictable and unsociable person, and then actually asked her if she wanted to become my wife, to which she gave the expected answer. I can hardly begin to describe the appalling experiences I endured in the following days. I decided that it must be my destiny and that I cannot escape it. So be it! God knows that my intentions towards my partner in life are of the best, and that if we are unhappy together it will be no fault of mine. If I marry without love it is only because circumstances have left me no alternative. I have never lied to her or deceived her in any way.

Tchaikovsky with his wife Antonina in 1877

Supposing he had, could he have deceived her as completely as she deceived herself? The marriage went ahead, on 18 July 1877, and was a catastrophe from the start.

There were only two witnesses: Tchaikovsky's brother Anatoly, and his friend Kotek (in point of fact, the true object of his love at that very time). Tchaikovsky himself was in a near-paralytic state of anxiety and grief – for himself, for his hapless wife, and also for their ill-starred future, together or apart:

> *I married not in accordance with the dictates of my heart, but because of a mixture of circumstances which I fail to understand and which led me, as though fated, to choose the most difficult of all options. No sooner did I find myself alone with my new wife than she ceased to inspire even simple friendship but became to me utterly detestable, in the fullest sense of the word. I was convinced that the best, perhaps the only good part of me – my musical talent – had now irretrievably perished. I could see nothing but a future of miserable vegetation, of living out, day by day, an entirely unbearable, oppressive farce. I fell at once into a deep despair, began passionately hungering for death, which seemed the only escape available to me. Yet for the sake of my family, I could not contemplate suicide. It would deal them a blow from which they would never recover. And anyway, my weakness (if such it is) is that I love life, I love my work, I love the successes awaiting me in the future. And finally, I have still not said all that I can and want to say before departing for eternity. So, Death has not yet taken me, nor when all is said and done am I really able to seek it. But what then remains to me? . . . Oh, I do not know why I did not go mad!*

'I saw my life before me, shattered. And I fell into despair. Today, the crisis seems to have passed. But, oh God it was terrible, terrible, terrible!'

In truth, he almost did; and as we know, not for the first time. A week after the wedding, he wrote to his brother Anatoly:

> *When I awoke, the morning after, I saw my life before me, shattered. And I fell into despair. Today, the crisis seems to*

have passed. But, oh God it was terrible, terrible, terrible! If it weren't for the great love I feel for you and my other dear ones, who stood by me while I endured the unendurable, it might have ended badly – in illness, even madness. But today – today I am beginning to recover.

The story, however, was only beginning. 'As time went on, my soul became filled with such a fierce hatred of my unfortunate wife that I wanted to strangle her.' And later: 'When I see her, my blood runs cold with horror! What can be more terrible than to behold with one's own eyes this most loathsome of nature's creations! Why do such reptiles exist at all!'

His wife seemed completely unaware of her husband's true feelings, and displayed a serene and exasperating refusal to perceive reality.

Yet in the midst of this living nightmare (and to Tchaikovsky's intense annoyance) his wife wore, in his own words, 'a perpetual expression of unalloyed happiness and contentment' and seemed completely unaware of her husband's true feelings. While acknowledging that all was not well in their relationship, she displayed a serene and exasperating refusal to perceive the reality of her situation:

What do all our trials, failures and difficulties amount to when compared with the power of my love for you and of your love for me! Come what may, I know that in your love I shall always find support and comfort. Even now, you are in my mind every second of the day and night and the very thought of your dear face consoles, encourages, and supports me.

Of their life together in Moscow that autumn, when Tchaikovsky was in mental torment, she reports:

> *Surreptitiously and unobserved, I was forever admiring him, especially when he was having his morning tea; he simply radiated freshness, always so beautiful, with his gentle eyes, that I was totally entranced by him. While gazing at him I would think to myself: 'Thank God! This man belongs to me and no one else! No one can take him away from me. He is my husband!'*

According to his friend Kashkin, Tchaikovsky decided to take his own life – but in such a way that no one would suspect suicide.

But Tchaikovsky could take himself away; and this, according to his friend Kashkin (who claimed to have had this news from the composer himself), is what he duly attempted to do. He decided, so Kashkin relates, to take his own life – but in such a way that no one would suspect suicide. That they never did suspect anything is due more to his naivety than to the ingenuity of his plan. On a cold September evening – so we read in biography after biography – Tchaikovsky waded into the icy waters of the Moscow River and immersed himself till his body was seized with cramps. On returning home, he explained, lamely, that he had stumbled and fallen into the river.

The plan was based on his unquestioning assumption that he would catch pneumonia and die. Such, however, was the strength of his constitution that he never even caught a cold. The story is unlikely to be true (it was related, in any case, many years after his death), but it is beyond doubt that Tchaikovsky was bent on escape in some form:

> *One thing is certain: that I never want to spend another day with Antonina Ivanovna! I would sooner agree to be tortured than ever to lay eyes on her again. It is quite preposterous to think that she can in some way be changed, transforming her into a suitable wife. To begin with, it is obviously mad for me to try to live with any wife. And even were it possible, it could never*

> *be with this one! I believe I have never met a more unpleasant human being. But how am I to be rid of her? One thing only do I know: I must disappear – for a year at the very least.*

This he proceeded, or attempted, to do. It was not, of course, a plan he confided to his wife, who recalled, rather pathetically:

> *One day, he simply informed me that he was being called away on business. For three days, I went with him to the mail train; his eyes were all over the place, he was obviously nervous, but my thoughts were far from any trouble that might be lying in wait for me. Before the first bell went, he suffered a spasm in his throat and went alone, with jerky, uncoordinated steps, to find a drink of water. Then we entered the carriage; he looked straight at me – sadly, but without lowering his eyes . . . And that was it. He never came back to me.*

The business, as it happens, was genuine. Tchaikovsky had been asked to go to St Petersburg in connection with a forthcoming revival of one his operas. Almost immediately upon his arrival, on September 25th, he suffered a devastating, yet providential, emotional collapse. A week or so later, on doctor's orders, he left Russia in the company of his brother Anatoly, arriving in Switzerland at the beginning of October to begin a lengthy convalescence. It was at this point that he began regularly to speak of his wife in terms of such violent hatred that he now referred to her almost exclusively as 'the reptile'. For the rest of his life, with one enduring exception, any mention or news of her would reduce him to a state of hysteria. The exception was his correspondence with Mme von Meck, in which they both studiously referred to Antonina as 'the certain individual', never risking the consequence of mentioning her name.

For the rest of his life, any mention or news of his wife would reduce him to a state of hysteria.

It was during his convalescence in Switzerland that Tchaikovsky wrote a long letter to Mme von Meck, virtually begging her for money while never actually saying as much:

> *It is terrible – painfully, tearfully difficult – but I must force myself to it, I must appeal to your apparently unending kindness. Do you not find it odd that fate should have brought us together at the very moment when, having committed a sequence of mad acts and decisions, I must turn to you with a direct request for your assistance?! . . . I fear that everybody must now look down on me for my faithlessness, weakness, and stupidity – and I am deathly afraid that even you may feel something close to contempt for me. But this is probably the voice of my chronic suspiciousness. I know that you realise, by instinct, that while I may be wretched, I am not a bad person. Oh my dear beloved friend! In the midst of my agonies in Moscow, when I felt that there was no escape for me but death, I confess the thought flashed through my mind sometimes that you might save me. When my brother took me abroad, seeing that I needed to be far away, I reflected again that without you I would probably be overwhelmed, unable to function, and that you would appear again as my saviour. As I write, I am racked by pangs of conscience, yet still know that you are my true friend, who can see into the innermost depths of my being, though we are only acquainted through letters.*

The pangs of conscience were richly earned. The letter is blatantly manipulative, but it had the desired effect. She replied by return of post.

> *My dear Pyotr Il'yich, why do you upset and wound me so by worrying overmuch about material things? Your anxiety clouds the great happiness I derive from looking after you and seems to suggest that we are not close to one another. Why do you suppose this is? It causes me much pain.*

With this same letter, in a separate note, which Tchaikovsky never preserved, Mme von Meck settled on him a lavish annuity of 6,000 roubles so that he could abandon his duties at the Conservatoire and from then on devote himself exclusively to composition. This exceeded his wildest expectations. His response was immediate and predictable.

> *My dear, my beloved friend,*
> *There are feelings that lie beyond words. Try as I might to express what you inspire in me, the result, I fear, would ring hollow. But then you have always read my heart. I will say only this: I never imagined, until knowing you, that there could be anyone with a spirit as infinitely tender and sublime as yours. I am as amazed at what you do for me as at how you do it. My most invaluable friend, I thank you for all this from the very bottom of my heart. Know that every note which flows from my pen from this moment on will be for you.*

Needless to say, this turn of events did nothing to hurt his recovery. Weeks rather than months later, he awoke one morning, looked around him with the kind of dazed relief that follows the escape from a nightmare, and could hardly believe his luck. 'Not only have I not perished, when that seemed the only possibility, but things are fine now, and the future is dawning in happiness and success.' Sooner than he could previously have imagined, he was able to review the events of the last few months with something approaching detachment:

> *When I think back on the crazy things I did, I can only conclude that I suffered an attack of temporary insanity from which I have now successfully emerged. Much of my recent past appears as a strange and violent nightmare in which someone who seemed to be me behaved as people do in dreams: senselessly, incoherently, wildly. This was not myself, exercising the normal resources of willpower in a reasonable and logical way. Everything I did bore the stamp of that terrible divorce between reason and will, which is, in truth, the mark of madness.*

Whether he had indeed been clinically insane remains debatable, but what is certain is that he had survived the worst crisis of his life, and emerged intact.

Interlude III: Tchaikovsky and the Orchestra

Tchaikovsky was first and foremost a man of the orchestra. If we knew him only by his chamber music, songs and solo piano music, the adjective 'great' would never have accompanied his name, though he would probably not have been forgotten. Unlike Mozart, Schubert, Mendelssohn, Brahms and Bizet, he was, as we have seen, something of a late starter, not beginning to compose until he was nearly fourteen, and not undertaking any serious study of harmony until he was twenty-one (Mozart, Schubert and Mendelssohn had written masterpieces when they were sixteen). By the age at which Tchaikovsky entered the St Petersburg Conservatoire most music students today have completed their formal studies; yet within two years of his entry he produced his first substantial work, an overture to Ostrovsky's play **The Storm**, which still warrants the occasional performance and recording. Indeed when one considers that it was only a year afterwards that he was invited to become a professor of harmony at the newly opened Moscow Conservatoire, his progress must be reckoned as little short of phenomenal.

His First Symphony, using a number of folk-like themes, has at times an almost operatic feel to it.

It was in Moscow that he composed his First Symphony (subtitled 'Winter Daydreams') in 1866. Using a number of folk-like themes, plus one authentic folksong which leads to the finale, the work has at times an almost operatic feel to it. As it turned out, it set the tone for his symphonies as a whole, excepting only the last.

Between this and the composition of his Second Symphony six years later, Tchaikovsky wrote his first orchestral masterpiece, the fantasy overture **Romeo and Juliet**, which remains one of the most popular of all orchestral works. Its richness of orchestration, abundance of beautiful, soaring melodies (particularly the great love theme), vivid characterisation and structural integrity immediately mark Tchaikovsky out as one of the major Russian composers of his time, if not already the finest. His only serious rivals were the self-styled nationalists Mussorgsky, Borodin and Rimsky-Korsakov, members of the so-called 'Mighty Handful', whose talent was not generally matched by a comparable degree of self-discipline and craftsmanship. In the case of Balakirev, whose bullying played such a major part in the ultimate success of *Romeo and Juliet*, it was rather the other way round. Anton Rubinstein, one of the most towering figures in the history of piano playing, was nowhere near Tchaikovsky's match when it came to sheer creative genius, though his best works are not to be sniffed at – some of them, such as the Fourth Piano Concerto, are still in the repertoire today, if only peripherally.

The fantasy overture *Romeo and Juliet*, one of the most popular of all orchestral works, marks Tchaikovsky as one of the major Russian composers of his time, if not already the finest.

Tchaikovsky felt his essential Russianness every bit as fervently as did the 'Mighty Handful', perhaps especially in the earlier part of his career, but he had none of their principled disdain for the highly schooled (and from their perspective stultifyingly 'academic') traditions of western European music. Ironically, however, it was precisely in Tchaikovsky's attempts to emulate the European symphonic ideal (Mozart, although his favourite composer, proved an elusive role model) that he demonstrated his greatest weaknesses as a composer. A man of the orchestra he indubitably was, but he was not by instinct a man of the symphony. Speaking very generally, his finest orchestral works are the ballets, programmatic overtures, tone poems, incidental music for the theatre, and the Serenade for strings. His symphonies, especially the last three, certainly contain great music, but all have come in for widespread censure as symphonic structures.

The essence of symphonic thought is organic and developmental. It has everything to do with the relationship of the proverbial acorn to the proverbial oak, or of the seed in the soil to the flower in sunlight. The most important thing about a theme in a symphony, as opposed to the melody of a folksong or an operatic aria, is not what it is but what it can become.

One of the most fundamental properties of a symphonic movement – of any piece in sonata form – is its capacity for suspense, manifested in the continual alternation of stability and flux. It raises questions: What happens next? How do we get out of here? Where, and to what, will we be taken? When, and how, will we get home? Every question begs an answer. Everything is focused on the future. This, together with the impulse towards symmetry, is the engine that drives the very concept of the symphony. Tchaikovsky's symphonies are largely fuelled by emotion and the senses, though not as disproportionately as is often claimed. Many of his themes are far more beautiful than anything in countless 'impeccable' symphonies by lesser men, and his use of the orchestra leaves most of his rivals at the starting gate. But so far from being seeds, Tchaikovsky's themes are often fully bloomed flowers: delectable, enveloping, seductively fragrant – and sometimes exasperatingly self-sufficient. They leave nothing to be desired.

Tchaikovsky's themes are often fully bloomed flowers: delectable, enveloping, seductively fragrant. They leave nothing to be desired.

No one was more aware of these 'limitations' than Tchaikovsky himself. 'All my life,' he wrote to a friend, 'I have been much troubled by my inability to grasp and manipulate form in music. What I write has always a mountain of padding. Any experienced eye can detect the thread in my seams, yet I can do nothing about it.' Part of his problem (though many musicians do not see it as one) lay in the very nature of his national heritage, enshrined in the traditions of Russian folk music. One of the principal hallmarks of folksong in general, and Russian folksong in particular, is its reliance on numerous repetitions, each one varied in some small – usually very small – way. But however many instrumental costume changes may assist it, this gradual, largely decorative process bears little relation to the form of organic evolution required in a symphony carved in the western classical tradition.

Tchaikovsky's Second Symphony abounds in attractive features and scored a great success at its first performance.

Tchaikovsky's **Second Symphony**, sometimes called the 'Little Russian' (after the old name for what is now Ukraine), was composed in 1873, when he was pushing thirty-four. The work is largely based on local folk tunes; in the last movement, however, Tchaikovsky carries repetition to near-suicidal extremes, giving us the same theme eighteen times before introducing any variation at all. Nevertheless, the work abounds in attractive features and scored a great success at its first performance.

Again, the gap between symphonies is filled, more comfortably, by works of non-specific form: some very substantial incidental music to Ostrovsky's fairy-tale **The Snow Maiden** (also from 1873), in which Tchaikovsky's powers of characterisation and atmosphere are very much to the fore, and an orchestral fantasy on a 'programme' derived from Shakespeare's play *The Tempest* (again from 1873). Virtually eclipsing both these works in popularity and durability, however, is the **Piano Concerto No. 1** in B flat minor (1874–5). Initially scorned by Nikolay Rubinstein as 'unplayable', it has long enjoyed a popularity rivalled only by Grieg's Piano Concerto in A minor (a work which Tchaikovsky admired) and Rachmaninov's in C minor. Long, big-boned and intentionally difficult to play, it combines dazzling bravura, high drama and sheer entertainment with a charming lyricism and a raft of good tunes, the first of which was hijacked and recycled as an American popular song, *Tonight We Love*.

Francesca da Rimini is hyper-romantic tone poem based on Dante's *Inferno* that for all its orchestral brilliance shows Tchaikovsky at his most recklessly emotional.

The Third Symphony, completed in 1875, finds Tchaikovsky drawing back from the folk-orientated styles of the first two and turning to European models (Schumann, in particular, is a strong influence); but even here he lapses into Russian repetitiousness. Far more successful in every sense are the intense, even melodramatic 'symphonic fantasia' *Francesca da Rimini* and its polar opposite, the lightweight and charming **Variations on a Rococo Theme** for cello and orchestra. Both works date from 1876, the year in which Tchaikovsky wrote to Modest of his decision to marry. *Francesca da Rimini* is a hyper-romantic tone poem, based on Dante's *Inferno*, and for all its orchestral brilliance it shows Tchaikovsky at his most recklessly emotional. His abiding problem as a composer, perhaps especially in his orchestral works, was not in fact his self-confessed inability to master form but a tendency to let his emotions run riot (though it must be said that this impression often derives as much, if not more, from the performers than from the composer). In *Francesca*, he only just manages to keep them in check.

Tchaikovsky first really hit his stride as a symphonist with his **Fourth Symphony** (1877–8), though it certainly has its flaws. The emotions are completely his own, being both eloquently expressed and well disciplined, and they are kept within the proportions of his chosen medium. The fact that he divulged an underlying programme to Mme von Meck (see page 90) but not to the listener at large may tell us more about his psychology than about the actual music. The work served to defuse the feelings of intimidation which he felt in the face of a 'pure' symphony and enabled him to 'feel' it more like an opera or a ballet. The themes are always well characterised and the orchestration is masterly from start to finish. The most famous movement is the exhilarating and high-spirited Scherzo, which Tchaikovsky had the inspired and unprecedented idea of scoring entirely for pizzicato strings, with the exception of the central 'trio' section which he gives to the winds. He may well have picked up the idea from the famous 'Pizzicati' number in Delibes' ballet *Sylvia*, which he certainly knew, or from the imitation of

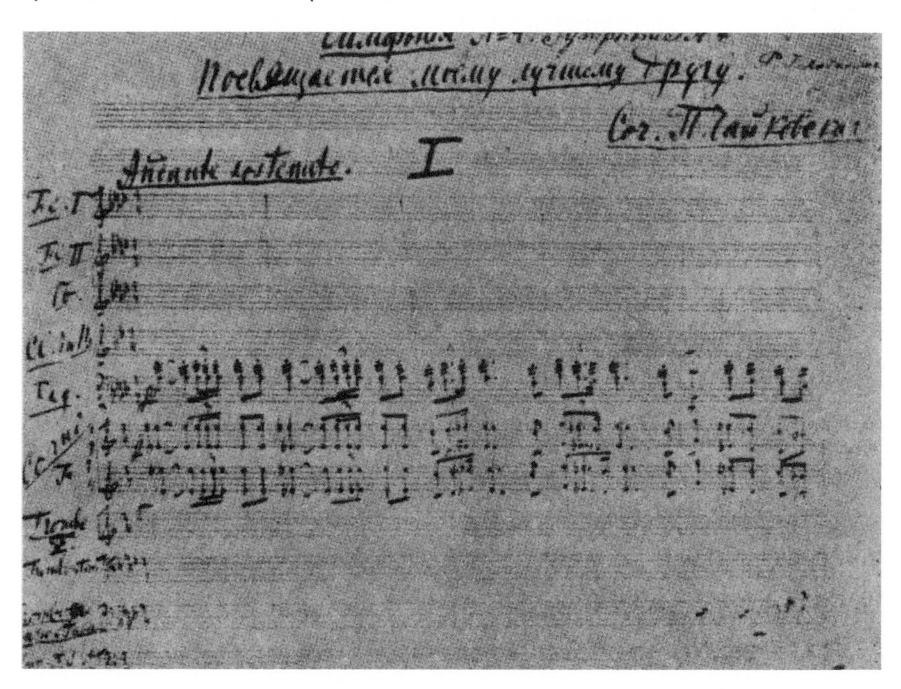

Manuscript of Tchaikovsky's Symphony No. 4, dedicated to Nadezhda von Meck

balalaikas in Glinka's opera *A Life for the Tsar*; but no one had ever thought of doing this kind of thing in a symphony, let alone on this scale. Despite the self-consciously fate-laden seriousness of the first movement and the poignant melancholy of the second, both the Scherzo and the finale are immensely enjoyable. The finale may sound more like a ballet than a symphony, despite the brief and unexpected reappearance of the 'fate' motif from the first movement, but with music of such freshness, charm and delectable colour, who's to complain? Many have, in fact, on the grounds just specified, but to what end? They have certainly not detracted one whit from the work's enduring popularity.

Before tackling his next symphony, Tchaikovsky turned once again to the form of the **concerto**, this time for the **violin** (1878). Here, particularly in the first movement, his supposed inability to master form goes out of the window. As Edward Garden has remarked, 'even Mozart might have approved'. The reckless emotionalism and occasionally gaudy orchestration that may be said to mar *Francesca da Rimini* are nowhere to be found here. Nor is there any trace of the trauma of his marriage, from which he seems to have emerged with a renewed, even enhanced joy in living and a mastery of his craft that could almost be described as serene (not a word that crops up often in discussions of Tchaikovsky's music). In his life, there was still much trauma to come, but this ebulliently lyrical work is at the very least an invigorating vision of what life might be. In its breadth and scope it bears comparison with the violin concertos of Beethoven and Brahms, both also in D major. (Interestingly, Brahms's Violin Concerto, which Tchaikovsky detested, was written at exactly the same time as his own.)

The original dedicatee of the Violin Concerto, Leopold Auer, refused to play.

Just as Nikolay had pronounced Tchaikovsky's First Piano Concerto 'unplayable', so history repeated itself when the original dedicatee of the Violin Concerto, Leopold Auer, refused to play it for the same reasons. Thus Tchaikovsky's two greatest concertos both received their first performances outside Russia. Adolph Brodsky premiered the Violin Concerto in Vienna, after which the critic Eduard Hanslick delicately ascribed to Tchaikovsky the invention of music that 'stinks to the ear'. It seems inconceivable that he could have applied this remark to the finale, which is one of the great feel-good showstoppers of the concerto repertoire. Tchaikovsky's other concerto works (including his two subsequent piano concertos, various movements for violin, and the *Pezzo capriccioso* for cello) are of secondary importance.

Adolph Brodsky, who premiered Tchaikovsky's Violin Concerto

All major works require major work, and after the exertions of the Fourth Symphony and the Violin Concerto, Tchaikovsky needed to cool the temperature a bit, to step back for a breather from the world of passion and emotion that was his normal stamping ground. His next work, the **Liturgy of St John Chrysostom**, is as close as he ever came to true asceticism. Its ritual economy and reserve are almost disturbing. In most of it the composer's personality seems to have been purged beyond recognition. With what feelings of regeneration and relief, then, must he have returned to the orchestra. All the orchestral works he produced between the Violin Concerto and the great *Manfred* symphony of 1885

are relatively lightweight and generally of minor significance, though none the less appealing for that. In effect, most of them are suites, by nature if not by name. All are attractive works and the orchestration is a joy, but their comparatively short movements rarely attempt to plumb any depths. The most popular pieces of this period are the brilliantly orchestrated and high-spirited **Capriccio italien** of 1880 (based, as its name suggests, on the popular music of Italy) and the **1812** festival overture of the same year, whose noisy battlescapes require everything but actual bombs. Many recorded versions do indeed marshal a battalion of cannon, complemented by the loudest church bells available. The work was an embarrassment to the composer, but it remains, with the possible exception of *The Nutcracker* suite, his number-one popular hit.

The most substantial orchestral work of this interim between symphonies is the **Serenade for strings** of 1881, one of Tchaikovsky's own special favourites. It arose neither from a commission nor because of any specific occasion but 'from inner compulsion'; and while it began life as a symphony it probably owes much of its quality to the abandonment of that idea, along with all its underlying baggage of intimidation, self-consciousness and self-doubt. Yet it has a greater degree of cohesion between movements and a more satisfying overall balance of ingredients than any of his formally designated symphonies so far. Among its cleverest strokes is the revelation, in the finale, of the Russian folksong on which the entire work has been based. Like so many of Tchaikovsky's most memorable themes, it consists largely of a simple descending scale – as does the opening of the work as a whole – which returns near the end of the finale to confirm its true paternity. Here

The *1812* festival overture was an embarrassment to the composer, but it remains, with the possible exception of *The Nutcracker* suite, his number-one popular hit.

again, Mozart might very well have approved. Tchaikovsky was now ready to embark on his most powerful symphonic work to date.

Perhaps because of its specific literary programme, Tchaikovsky did not include the **Manfred** symphony (1885) – based directly on Byron's eponymous tragedy – in the numbered sequence of his other symphonies, which is only one of the probable reasons why it remains markedly less known. No other composition cost Tchaikovsky so much labour or left him so exhausted. It was conceived on a massive scale (it runs to an hour or more) and its powerfully gloomy outer movements frame a scherzo – which depicts with extraordinary delicacy the Fairy of the Alps glimpsed in a rainbow through the spray of a waterfall – and a beautiful, idyllic pastorale, evoking the simplicity of Alpine life. The orchestration is unobtrusively virtuosic, and the cohesion of all four movements is remarkably self-assured. Balakirev, among others (including the composer), regarded this as Tchaikovsky's greatest work yet.

Before embarking on his far more familiar Fifth Symphony, Tchaikovsky in 1887 produced another orchestral suite, *Mozartiana*, a felicitous arrangement of piano pieces by his beloved Mozart. The **Fifth Symphony** appeared in the following year. Again there is an underlying programme, but nothing as specific as in *Manfred*. Nevertheless, it follows the example of the earlier work by introducing its 'motto' theme into each of its four movements, but with far more pervasive effect. There has always been criticism that the work is more like a cyclical opera than a symphony, and that its finale is misconceived and dramatically hollow, but even if it is justified the power of Tchaikovsky's music transcends its limitations, and the work has been a staple of the concert repertoire from his time to our own.

Happily, most commentators agree with Tchaikovsky himself that his sixth and last symphony, nicknamed

CD 2
track 12
.naxosbooks.com

'Pathétique' (1893), is perhaps the greatest of his works, and many would say the most dramatic, his operas notwithstanding. In terms of instrumentation alone, it stands as the summation of everything Tchaikovsky had learned about the orchestra, applied so perfectly to its expressive purpose that it is impossible to separate one from the other. Structurally it is as unconventional as anything else he wrote (it includes a waltz with five beats to the bar instead of three, and ends with a long slow movement of almost unmitigated tragedy), yet nothing he did was ever more convincing or more extreme. The dynamic range goes from the almost inconceivably soft (*pppppp*) to the almost intolerably powerful. The range of emotions is authentically terrifying yet is deployed with unerring control and dramatic conviction. There is not a wasted note or a misjudged chord from first to last. The sense of inevitability is achieved with an economy of means that is in no way ascetic, and at times the characterisation of themes is almost cruel in its intensity. In addition to its intrinsic quality, Tchaikovsky's last symphony, which was also his last work, has had a crucial influence on such disparate composers as Mahler, Berg, Sibelius, Puccini and Stravinsky. For one who was 'not a man of the symphony', this is no mean achievement.

Chapter 4

Sex, Suffering, Sublimation and Loss 1878–1884

Sex, Suffering, Sublimation and Loss 1878–1884

It would be stretching a point to say that Tchaikovsky's was a split personality in the normally accepted psychiatric sense, but such was the speed with which he could veer from one extreme to another that the layman could be forgiven for having that impression. On the subject of Venice, for instance, his feelings would seem to have been unequivocal:

> *If I were forced to be in such a city as this for as much as a week, I would hang myself in sheer despair by the fifth day. Apart from the Piazza San Marco, on which everything is centred, the rest is a maze of stinking passageways that lead nowhere – and unless you plant yourself in a gondola and order yourself to be taken about, you can't have the slightest notion of where you are. Boating along the Grand Canal is all right, as there are palaces (and palaces, and yet more palaces), all of marble and each one better than the last, yet at the same time filthier and more dilapidated. The Doges' Palace, I must admit, has much of beauty and interest, with its romantic aura of the Council of Ten, the Inquisition, tortures, oubliettes, and other like delights. Still, I went through it three times and, to clear my conscience, visited two or three churches with a veritable sea of paintings by Titian and Tintoretto, statues by Canova, and all sorts of admitted aesthetic gems. But the city itself is*

the very epitome of gloom, as if it had been deserted. There are no horses anywhere, as far as I can make out, nor have I seen a single dog.

But only a little time later, he reports:

I am completely transported by the charms of this wonderful city! I have been tearing about the place all day long in unfettered delight! And with every new day I discover yet more joys. We went recently to the church of the Frari, which, amongst a host of other beautiful things, contains Canova's mausoleum – a perfect miracle of beauty!

Paris, by contrast, captivated him from the start: 'In general, life here is extremely pleasant. You can do anything you like. The only thing you can't do is be bored! You have only to step out onto the boulevards and you feel cheerful at once.' But, as ever, it all depended: 'The first thing,' he wrote some time later, 'is that I really don't want to go to Paris. I find it a sickening place. It bores me so! Truth to tell, I would rather go to prison than to Paris.'

What applied to places, applied also to people. As we have seen, Tchaikovsky was a man whose frequently extreme statements should never be taken at face value, whether they refer to trivialities or life itself. For almost every view, you can find its exact opposite – if not in speech, then in behaviour. If Tchaikovsky had really been the misanthrope he often claimed to be, if he truly despised the human race, then he was not only a master of deceit but an inveterate masochist. As one friend wrote:

Tchaikovsky was a man whose frequently extreme statements should never be taken at face value.

His hospitality was boundless. Thus, for instance, when he was honoured with a serenade while travelling abroad, he promptly invited all the participants to dinner, and entertained them royally, without a thought of the expense. Playing host to his friends, too, often appeared to give him the greatest pleasure, and again, with no consideration of the cost. His attitude to money was simply incomprehensible to anyone practical. But that's how he was.

CD 1
track 10
www.naxosbooks.com

Website
www.naxosbooks.com

With the floodgates of his creativity now reopened, Tchaikovsky returned to composition refreshed and invigorated. By the beginning of the new year, 1878, he had put the finishing touches to his **Fourth Symphony**, the first of his works to be dedicated to his new guardian angel. The work itself, however, reflects far more of the trauma surrounding his marriage than of his emergence at the hands of Mme von Meck. Typically, Tchaikovsky had ambivalent feelings about the Romantic mania for so-called 'programme music', but for the sake of Mme von Meck he sketched out one for 'our symphony', as he always called it. Thus we learn that the very opening music is the 'Fate' motif, which is 'the germ of the whole symphony' (a claim difficult to substantiate analytically). He compared it to 'the sword of Damocles, that hangs over our heads'. The main theme of the first movement conveys feelings of 'hopelessness and depression.' The secondary theme represents 'escape from reality into a world of dreams', etc. But these moods are so clear from the music itself that an explanatory 'programme' is ultimately superfluous.

Tchaikovsky had ambivalent feelings about the Romantic mania for so-called 'programme music'.

By general consent, the greatest of Tchaikovsky's works from this period – and one that was intimately bound up with the fiasco of his marriage – is the most famous, and many believe the finest, of all his operas: *Eugene Onegin*. The relationship between circumstance and musical creation is notoriously difficult to define. As noted in the melodramatic *Francesca da Rimini* then the lightweight *Variations on a Rococo Theme*, Tchaikovsky, like Mozart, had a knack for composing polar opposites in response to a single event. In many ways, the turbulent, tortured passions of the Fourth Symphony seem to inhabit a different world entirely from the elegant, unhurried (though also tragic) *Onegin*. From the beginning, Tchaikovsky was worried that his adaptation of Pushkin's most famous novel would have too little action to find favour with audiences. As remarked earlier, he was careful to bill it not as an opera at all but as 'Lyrical or Elegiac Scenes'. However, this was never, or at least not primarily, an opera designed for others. It was something he had to write for himself, and he claimed while composing it that if it failed to enter the repertory it would hardly bother him. But when it was finished he was singularly impatient to have it published and staged as soon as possible. In the event, it was first produced semi-privately in 1879 at the Moscow Conservatoire. Its first public performance, again in Moscow, was a year later, when it had a very lukewarm reception from critics and audience alike.

In the opinion of many people, including Prokofiev and Stravinsky, *Eugene Onegin* is the most Russian opera ever written.

Tchaikovsky may not have been one of the 'Mighty Handful', with their principled nationalism, but in the opinion of many people, including Sergey Prokofiev and Igor Stravinsky, **Eugene Onegin** is the most Russian opera ever written. The influence of folk music is plainly there, not at all as an injection of nationalistic spice, but as a means of enhancing the difference in character between pastoral and urban life. Tchaikovsky's best operas were the ones in which he could most closely identify with the characters, and the parallels here were both close and obvious. Like Onegin himself, he had recently received an impassioned love letter from a young woman who hardly knew him, and it seems

Tchaikovsky in 1879

to have been Tatyana's letter scene in Pushkin's novel that persuaded him to take on the opera (his first impulse had been to set the scene separately, as a self-contained concert aria). But perhaps the greatest aria of all is the one in which Lensky, who is shortly to be killed by the caddish Onegin in a duel, reflects on his life, his former happiness and his present indifference as to whether he lives or dies.

From the very outset, the Violin Concerto flowed like oil. He was in top form, and exhilarated.

With the completion of the Fourth Symphony and *Onegin*, Tchaikovsky had paid his musical debts to the recent past, and could now turn to the future. The first thing that took shape in his mind was the **Violin Concerto** (see page 82). From the very outset, the composition flowed like oil. He was back in top form, and exhilarated in a way he hadn't been for many months. Within a surprisingly short time he was able to announce: 'The first movement of the Violin Concerto is already done. From the moment the right frame of mind came to me, it has never left me. With one's inner life in such a state, composing ceases altogether to be work: it becomes an unalloyed pleasure.'

For all his optimism at the time, however, he was by no means out of the woods where the trauma of his marriage was concerned. Well over a year after finishing the Violin Concerto he continued to suffer bouts of social paralysis that all but disabled him. The singer Alexandra Panayeva, already well known as a champion of his music, first met him at a dinner party in 1879:

> *The whole company assembled, and strained conversation was maintained in the drawing room until dinner. Pyotr Il'yich, looking totally confused and with eyes lowered, sat between his brothers, who never took their eyes off him. At dinner it was exactly the same . . . Afterwards, everyone moved to the reception room and, having conversed in a whisper about*

> *something, Anatoly Il'yich asked me to sing. Pyotr Il'yich sat at the piano. I went to the instrument, but the brothers asked me to stand a little further off, while they themselves sat like guards on either side of the composer. The latter turned quietly to his brother: 'Tolya, ask her to sing some Mozart.' In his turn Anatoly Il'yich turned to me: 'Pyotr Il'yich is asking for some Mozart,' he reported. I sang an aria from* The Marriage of Figaro *and Pamina's aria from* The Magic Flute. *Pyotr Il'yich was silent for a moment, sighed, dropped his hands onto his knees, and in a voice barely audible said: 'How nice.' Then: 'Modya, ask her for something else.' The twins turned to me in unison, beaming: 'He liked it, and asks you to sing something more.' Very gradually he became livelier, but continued to communicate his wishes and impressions only to his brothers, who eventually bore him away.*

By the time his father died, early in the following year, Tchaikovsky's condition had improved, though not dramatically. That his father's death occasioned sorrow rather than deep grief reflects the older man's circumstances rather than Tchaikovsky's. Il'ya Petrovich had lived a full, predominantly happy life, had enjoyed robust good health right into old age, marrying for a third time in his late seventies, and had died, without suffering, after a short illness at the age of eighty-four. Tchaikovsky, while always feeling filial affection for him, had never venerated him as he had his mother. Their relationship had been close rather than intimate, and Tchaikovsky was not dissembling when he wrote to Mme von Meck from Rome:

> *I bore my family sorrow without too great a shock. Time toughens us and we grow accustomed to such losses. Still, I am dreadfully sad to think that I will never see my dear father again. But the tears I have shed for this pure old man, with his angelic spirit, have affected me for the good, leaving*

my heart with a sense of enlightenment and reconciliation.

In the same letter we find again a striking contrast between the character of the music he was writing and the state of his mind at the time. A little later he reports:

> *I remain in the same nervous, irritable state as before. I am sleeping wretchedly and have generally been falling to pieces. However, for the last few days I have been working very well and have already completed the sketches for an Italian Fantasia on folk tunes, which I suspect may have a very bright future. It will be highly effective thanks to the enchanting tunes, which I've collected partly from albums, and partly just by listening on the streets.*

As ever, Tchaikovsky's enthusiasm for Italy waned, and his thoughts turned, almost obsessively, to Russia. In this regard he never changed: 'I like travelling abroad for relaxation; it is the greatest of pleasures. But I could live only in Russia. Only by living somewhere else do you realise how much, despite all its faults, you love our dear country.' But once back in that dear country? 'It's a strange thing. When I am in Russia, I dream, from morning until evening, even at night, about going abroad as soon as possible. Wherever I am, I seem to yearn to leave it. Nowhere am I at home. I am a *nomad*.'

'Wherever I am, I seem to yearn to leave it. Nowhere am I at home. I am a *nomad*.'

One of the distinct appeals of travelling was that, depending on the place, he could largely avoid being accosted by acquaintances (or admirers who would like to be acquaintances). There is a story he used to tell against himself, which he professed to find very amusing. It seems that he was walking down a street, far from Russia, when a lady cried out delightedly, in Russian, 'Why, Pyotr Il'yich! What a wonderful surprise!' Note the absence of surname. 'I am sorry, Madam,' he instantly replied, also in Russian, 'but you are mistaken. I am not Tchaikovsky.' And he continued on his way.

Wherever he went, Tchaikovsky indulged his flair for spending money. One cannot doubt for a moment that Mme von Meck's financial support had in some ways corrupted him. He took too much for granted, and he knew it:

> *From Mme von Meck I have received letters and an invitation to come to her estate at Braïlov, but without so much as a mention of any unusual payments. Meanwhile, I am filled with horror when I remember my debts and realise that until October I shan't have a kopek. Oh how spoiled I have become! And how dreadfully remiss in appreciating all that I owe to that wonderful woman.*

On the loose in the streets of Paris, however, thoughts of 'that wonderful woman' proved powerless against his spendthrift nature. In that respect he was no different from the man-about-town of his early Moscow days. 'Oh how you'd laugh if you could see me now!' he wrote to Anatoly in 1879:

> *I amble through the streets in a new grey overcoat and the most stylish top hat imaginable, flaunting a silk shirtfront with a coral pin at my neck, and lilac gloves on my hands. When passing the mirrored piers on the rue de la Paix, or on the boulevards, I cannot but pause to admire myself. Nor can I walk past a shop window without ogling the reflection of my elegance! Generally speaking, I have been overcome (as so often) by a positive mania of coquetry. I've had a new suit of clothes made, and ordered a dozen shirts. The money simply flies – even while I know that in a few days my pockets will be empty.*

Tchaikovsky's wife was beginning to show signs of a mental imbalance and was becoming increasingly paranoid.

In the meantime, Antonina tormented him by alternately accepting and refusing a divorce, at one stage making his life intolerable by moving into the flat above his. She was now also beginning to show signs of a mental imbalance greater than her husband's, and was becoming increasingly paranoid. For long stretches she would leave him alone, then suddenly break her silence with letters that drove him to the brink of another emotional collapse:

> *I do not wish to be even nominally the wife of a man who so viciously slanders a woman who has never done him the slightest harm. Why did you not start with yourself, and tell of your own terrible vice, before proceeding to judge me? And after all this, you have the gall to stress in your letters how kind and generous you are! But where are these qualities to be perceived, and how are they confirmed? Please do not take the trouble to answer me. Everything is finished between us, and I therefore beseech you, dear sir, not to indulge in lengthy correspondence but to deal only with this matter. And once again I repeat that I shall sign no filthy and untrue papers.*

By this time, her letters were badly unsettling Tchaikovsky before they were even opened: 'There is in this person, in her very handwriting, some poison that has a devastating effect on me! At the mere sight of the address written in her hand, I at once begin to feel sick – both morally and physically sick!'

But she continued to erupt, unpredictably, into his life, and the idea of divorce was eventually abandoned on both sides. When it was later discovered that she had given birth to an illegitimate child Tchaikovsky had all the grounds necessary to divorce her, but he was by now too wearied by her war of attrition to pursue the matter. It must be said, too, that he was acutely aware that his homosexuality would become public knowledge all over the world if the case should ever come to court. It never did. They remained married but unreconciled. After giving birth to a host of illegitimate children, each deposited in a foundling's home, Antonina spent the last twenty years of her life in a mental hospital, where she died, twenty-four years after her husband, in 1917 – the year of the Bolshevik Revolution.

Tchaikovsky not in emotional turmoil would hardly have been Tchaikovsky.

Tchaikovsky not in emotional turmoil (at least in prospect) would hardly have been Tchaikovsky. Almost as soon as he returned to Russia in the year following his father's death he was enveloped in another crisis, this one precipitated by the drafting into the Russian army in October of his long-standing personal servant (and lover), Alyosha Sofronov. No one close to Tchaikovsky could doubt that this was much more than just the loss (and the temporary loss, at that) of a servant. It was an event that brought him yet again to the brink of a nervous breakdown and it had a serious effect on his creative life. Indeed, the crisis began before it was even confirmed that the drafting would go ahead. The decision on that front was to be made by drawing lots. All those concerned had been summoned to attend the procedure in Moscow. Before Alyosha's departure, Tchaikovsky confided to Mme von Meck:

I am living in terrible suspense. Tomorrow or the next day, Alyosha departs. His going will not be easy for me. To lose someone with whom you have lived for fully a decade . . . is difficult indeed. I confess to pitying myself, but mostly I pity him. He will have to endure much hardship before he grows accustomed to his new situation. I have been working with exceptional intensity in an attempt to suppress the sadness that wells up within me.

To begin with, the strategy was broadly successful, but Alyosha's departure left it in ruins:

> *O my dear, my beloved Alyosha! How dreadfully poorly I have felt since you went. I cannot help thinking how much easier I would find all this if you were with me! Come what may, just remember that you will always be mine, whether you're drafted or whether you're not. Never, ever, shall I forget you, not for one second. If fate does indeed decree that you must enter the army, then I shall count every day, impatiently awaiting your return to me. I kiss you warmly and embrace you with all my heart, and feelings of the deepest tenderness.*

Fate, as he had feared, decided against him. His defences collapsed. Some days later he reported to Modest, 'Alyosha has been drafted. I can bear it only because I am constantly drinking. If it were not for continual dinners and suppers with drink I believe I should literally go mad.' Once again, he came perilously close. He sought out Alyosha in his barracks, where he found him as miserable as he had imagined. He arranged to be in Moscow as often as he could, expressly for the purpose of being with Alyosha whenever possible, demeaning himself in attempts to win favours for his 'little soldier', as he called him, 'weeping much', and growing strangely indifferent to the adulation in which he was increasingly held, by the public at large and the musical establishment in particular. Solely to dull the pain of Alyosha's absence, he continued, sporadically, to drink himself into oblivion. Time brought little comfort. Long after Alyosha's induction, Tchaikovsky wrote to him:

> *Every evening, when I have undressed, I sit at my desk and begin to grieve and pine, lamenting the fact that you are not*

> *beside me. I know it sounds ridiculous, but I weep at the very sight of anything that reminds me of you. No one can ever replace you, my dear Alyosha. I embrace you with all my heart.*

New misfortunes, or the threat of them, now began to crowd in upon him. The death of Nikolay Rubinstein at the age of only forty-five, in March 1881, shook him deeply, though it briefly lifted the creative lethargy that had overtaken him. Almost the only work he managed to produce that year was an immensely long **piano trio** which he intended as an instrumental requiem for Rubinstein, and which has been in the mainstream chamber repertoire ever since.

Almost the only work he managed to produce that year, an immensely long piano trio, has been in the mainstream chamber repertoire ever since.

During the composition of this work, rumours reached Tchaikovsky that Mme von Meck had suffered a severe financial crisis and was selling some of her several properties in an attempt to forestall impending bankruptcy. He wrote to her directly:

> *My freedom and the luxurious material existence that I lead are blessings beyond valuation. But if I were to learn that I enjoy them to the detriment of the most tactful and generous friend any man could have, they would at once become burdensome to me. Speaking without any exaggeration, I owe you my life. And so, my dear friend, for God's sake do not conceal the truth from me. There is nothing I desire more than your own wellbeing. Any pleasure that does damage to your interests is instantly poisoned for me. If you are indeed obliged to reduce your expenses, then let me too change my way of life and return to the conservatoires, where I would be joyfully welcomed.*

The lady would have none of it. 'Why take on again that heavy yoke? Your nerves and health are only just beginning to settle down, to grow stronger, and now again all will be ruined and lost. *I shall not give up my right to take care of you*, nor have *you* the right to take it from *me* – until such time,' she added, perhaps a little ominously, 'as I am no longer able to enjoy it.'

In the meantime, Tchaikovsky himself found considerable joy in the news that his eighteen-year-old niece Vera was engaged to be married. Her fiancé was a young naval officer whose name, by pure coincidence, happened to be Nikolay Rimsky-Korsakov – exactly the same as that of the composer, who, though no relation, was also a naval officer. On a visit to the family home at Kamenka, where he often stayed, Tchaikovsky met the happy couple for the first time. But as he reported to Modest, the pleasure, on his part, was distinctly bittersweet:

> *How much in love the young man is! Just as I used to be. He devours dear Vera with his eyes, is angry and anguished as soon as she leaves him for a moment. But one can see that this is not merely infatuation, but genuine, normal love. Oh, Modya, what poor devils we are, you and I – for we shall live out our entire lives without experiencing, even for a single second, the full, true happiness of normal love.*

His tragedy was ultimately not his homosexuality but his unfulfilled yearning for a stable relationship.

The reflection made him sadder still. (His tragedy was ultimately not his homosexuality but his unfulfilled yearning for a stable relationship, though obviously he saw a connection.) But at least he recovered the will to work, if not the joy of it. For more than a year, the creative flame had seemed to desert him. He had busied himself, instead, with a commission from his publisher, editing the church music of

Dmitry Bortnyansky, music which he frankly admitted he 'loathed'. In December he reported to Mme von Meck that he had begun work on a new opera, *Mazeppa*. But the spark was gone. 'I work conscientiously, yes,' he wrote, 'but without enthusiasm, nor with even a fraction of the inspiration and love for my nascent creation that I have known in former times.'

Mme von Meck, in the meantime, had more pressing concerns. With characteristic shrewdness – and toughness – she had managed to reverse the decline in her fortunes, regaining much of her lost wealth. Her health, perhaps in consequence of the cumulative strain, was failing: she had begun to develop acute pains in her right hand, leaving her unable to write more than a few lines at a time, and even those with difficulty. Nor, it seems, could the doctors ease her distress: 'No remedies help,' she reported. 'None. And my condition steadily worsens. The bitterest thing for me in all this, however, is the thought that I will be deprived of conversing with you, my dear, my only friend. With you I have unburdened my heart, rested, recompensed myself for much of the grief I have had from life, and to lose this sole consolation is very acutely painful to me.'

Inevitably, their correspondence dwindled, and not only on her side. Without the stimulus of her letters to answer, Tchaikovsky slowed from an average of one every other day (sometimes even one a day), to one a week, one every ten days, one a month. In time, especially when he was particularly busy, several months might elapse without his writing to her – yet throughout this time he continued to communicate regularly with his family. The 'affair', one of the strangest in the history of art, was beginning to cool.

Interlude IV:
The Chamber Music

Tchaikovsky's chamber music occupies a very small portion of his output, numbering little more than eight works. Among its most surprising features is the fact that the highest (or at least the most sustained) degree of mastery is found in the very first full-length chamber work he wrote (barring a lost student work): his **String Quartet in D major, Op. 11**, composed in 1871. Its slow movement, which has earned a popularity all its own, moved Tolstoy to tears and has since had a similar (if not so extreme) effect on many others. As with Rachmaninov and his C sharp minor Prelude, the movement became for a time Tchaikovsky's best-known piece (whether in its original form or in countless arrangements). The point was reached where he almost regretted having written it. Given that the string quartet is a famously exacting medium and that Tchaikovsky was totally inexperienced as a string player, the strictly musical (as opposed to the popular) success of this quartet is truly remarkable. The polyphonic writing is both clear and supple, the subtly different character of the various instruments is sensitively exploited, the themes are equally natural, and the pacing of the whole work is masterly. The main theme of the famous second movement is one of the most beautiful Russian folksongs, previously unknown to

The highest degree of mastery is found in his very first full-length chamber work, his String Quartet in D major.

Russians at large, and sketched by Tchaikovsky after hearing a peasant sing it in the countryside. Tchaikovsky's treatment of it is correspondingly simple, which is probably one of the secrets of the quartet's popularity. However, when a composer writes a piece that continues to resonate in the hearts and minds of millions of listeners, through many generations, and all over the world, he just may have captured something important that his more 'sophisticated' critics have missed. Sticking power of this order is no accident.

The Second Quartet, Op. 22 followed three years later, in 1874, and though it too was an instant success (even with the generally vindictive César Cui) it failed to maintain prominence because it lacks its predecessor's consistency. A more openly ambitious work (evident from the start in its imposing, chromatic introduction), it was one of Tchaikovsky's own favourite progeny; but like much of his piano music it suffers from excessively 'orchestral' textures, especially in the finale. As is the case with the First Quartet, its heart is the slow movement, which similarly combines simplicity with an enchanting poignancy. Except for the rather 'orchestral' middle section of this slow movement, the writing throughout the work is in true quartet style.

The Second Quartet was one of Tchaikovsky's own favourite progeny.

There is an abidingly elegiac feel to the Third Quartet, Op. 80. It was written in 1876 in memory of the Czech violinist Ferdinand Laub, who had died a year earlier, and rather appropriately there is often a Dvořákian feel to it. Among its more Czech features is the degree and kind of its rhythmic variety, which alternates between foursquare stateliness and complex webs of combined rhythmic patterns that keep the music moving along, sometimes with surprisingly minimal melodic activity. In many ways, this is the most interesting of the three quartets as there is so much to listen to. The first movement is a striking case in point. Indeed, Tchaikovsky could be criticised for allowing so much to happen to his themes during the exposition that when the formal development section is reached it can seem almost redundant. Particularly noticeable in this quartet (and also in the earlier two) is Tchaikovsky's fondness for pedal points: long, sustained notes in the bass that underpin and prolong the harmony while imparting an extra degree of freedom to the melodic activity above. An interesting feature in the recapitulation is the surprising appearance of an entirely new theme before the expected return of the second subject. The Scherzo, again placed second, is attractive and accomplished, if less eventful, and the slow movement (once more the heart of the work) is deeply felt, though some may find it lachrymose to the point of sentimentality. The finale is by general consent the weakest movement, with more bustle than inspiration. For the remainder of his life Tchaikovsky wrote no further quartets. There are, however, five earlier quartet movements, composed between 1863 and 1865; slight works, they nevertheless make for pleasant and diverting listening.

Tchaikovsky's Piano Trio was composed 'in memory of a great artist', Nikolay Rubinstein.

Tchaikovsky's next chamber work, the **Piano Trio**, was composed 'in memory of a great artist', namely Nikolay Rubinstein, who died in 1881 at the age of forty-five. The relationship between the composer and his mentor/tormentor had been complicated, to say the least, but it does account for the unusual prominence of the piano and the almost bewilderingly wide range of emotions expressed. The work is technically in two movements, the second being a sprawling set of variations that includes a fugue and a vast summation (topping eleven minutes), which ends in funereal mood and amounts in effect to a third movement. Much of the time, it sounds like a piano concerto with an accompanying orchestra

of two rather than a piece of chamber music. It probably reflects Tchaikovsky's inner (albeit ambivalent and partially guilty) sense of relief as strongly as his sense of loss. The work remains in the repertoire, but few beyond impassioned Tchaikovskyans lay claim to loving it.

His next, and last, chamber work is a far more attractive affair with a prevailing bonhomie that belies its birth pangs. 'I have started a string sextet,' Tchaikovsky wrote in 1890, 'and am having dreadful difficulties with it: I constantly feel that I haven't got six real parts at all, that I'm actually writing for orchestra and *rearranging* it for six string instruments. But maybe it will go better when I've got the hang of things.' It did indeed go better, but it comes as no surprise that the piece is today far better known as an orchestral work. This bubblingly good-natured, four-movement work (its cheeriness conveyed, unusually but infectiously, in the minor mode) was conceived in Italy, hence its title *Souvenir de Florence*. But it is Russian to the core despite the inclusion of a few Italianisms, a profligate melodiousness, and rather Germanic self-control. It makes a strangely inconclusive end to Tchaikovsky's chamber career, for very agreeable though the *Souvenir* is, it is without any real sense of culmination.

Chapter 5

House, Home and Happiness 1885–1888

House, Home and Happiness 1885–1888

Tchaikovsky's desire for a new and stable home had been growing for some years. For two decades he had moved from pillar to post, renting various properties, living in hotels or, more often, staying with members of his family and relying on them to look after him. In his mid-forties he was developing a conscience. Yet for all his natural generosity of spirit, he remained, like most great creative artists, essentially self-centred:

> *It has slowly begun to dawn upon me that I am too old to continue being a sponger. I have reached the point where, all last evening, for instance, I sulked, selfishly, because chicken was served for dinner and some other dish was cancelled and replaced by yoghurt. And there are a thousand other trifles, equally revealing of my sponging nature. This will become completely intolerable if I don't settle down in a place of my own.*

At last, he began to do something about it, but cautiously and in stages. Barring foreign journeys, he would live from then on within the boundaries of one district in the countryside, though he failed to find the necessary solace in a single house. He continued to occupy a sequence of dwellings, but in each he preserved exactly the same arrangement of the same furniture, fittings and contents in every room, and exactly the same placement of paintings and photographs on the walls. The first house he took was outside the village of Maidanovo, near the city of Klin, and it was here that he mapped out a daily routine from which he almost never departed, except when abroad. As the daughter of a close friend reports:

> *He rose between seven and eight, and bathed in the river that flowed right past the house (where the bathing was excellent). After his morning tea he devoted some time either to studying English or to serious reading. This was followed by the first of his daily walks, this lasting no more than three quarters of an hour. From half past nine until one he worked. At one o'clock precisely, he had lunch, after which, whatever the weather, he took another walk. He had read somewhere that two hours of walking a day were essential to one's health, and observed this rule religiously. Solitude during these walks was essential, for he spent most of the time composing in his head. By four o'clock he returned home for afternoon tea. At this time he would read through the papers or converse with his guests, if he had any. From five until seven he worked at his desk. Before supper, in the summer, he took yet a third walk, this time, very often, in the company of friends, while in autumn or winter he usually played the piano, alone – or in duets, if he had musicians visiting. And after supper, until eleven, a game of cards, some reading, or writing letters, of which there were always very many.*

He corresponded regularly in four or five languages, and while he often failed to return a book or an object that he had borrowed, he almost never left a letter unanswered. His study of English is interesting. Though he had read numerous works of English

Tchaikovsky corresponded regularly in four or five languages, and almost never left a letter unanswered.

literature in translation, and based a number of compositions on some of them (as indeed he was about to do again), the spur to learning the language properly was actually his desire to read Dickens in the original. Among the most touching and amusing of his letters to his family is the first (and last) in English, written some time earlier:

The spur to learning the English language properly was actually his desire to read Dickens in the original.

My good sister and my dear brother!
I have known what mötsch plesir that you learn Englisch language; böt you cannot told that I cannot understand. I kan understand wery biutföll oll what you will and enough bether. My brother! You are one fulischmen, böt you, my dear sister, are one biutifföll women. I have not time to scrive this letter englisch, böt God sawe the Quenn and collection of Britisch autors is one trifles . . . Do not argue with me, You argue against reason and I abide by what I say . . .
I are your
Affectioned brother,
Pither

The first work composed in his new home was a piece he had been pondering for some time – a programmatic symphony based on Byron's poetic drama **Manfred**.

It was bound to demand a huge amount of energy and concentration, because it was a highly serious and complex undertaking. The moment I began work on it, it utterly engaged my enthusiasm. I found it quite impossible to put aside. But it meant a summer of almost unremitting melancholy and nervous strain, since the subject matter is so depressing. Never before have I put so much effort into a piece. Nor have I ever found composing so exhausting.

Immediately upon completing the work, Tchaikovsky returned to an opera, *The Sorceress*, which had been effectively sidelined by the *Manfred* symphony. In May of 1886, after an exceptionally long time at home, he revisited Paris and then spent a happy month in Tiflis (now Tbilisi, Georgia) with his brother Anatoly. By the end of June he was back at Maidanovo, where he finished *The Sorceress* – except for the orchestration, which, unusually, took him another nine months. In January 1887, and then again in March, he conducted concerts of his own works in Russia and their success finally persuaded him to accept long-standing invitations to conduct similar concerts abroad. After the first four performances of *The Sorceress*, which to his thorough disappointment was not a success, he travelled west to begin his first-ever conducting tour outside Russia. He appeared, and was rapturously received, in Leipzig, Hamburg, Berlin, Prague, Paris and London (where he had his first opportunity to make daily use of his newly improved English).

Tchaikovsky conducted concerts of his own works in Russia and their success finally persuaded him to accept long-standing invitations to conduct similar concerts abroad.

It was also on this tour that Tchaikovsky first met Brahms. Given his dislike and intemperate abuse of Brahms's music, he was pleasantly surprised by the man himself:

> *Brahms is rather a short man, and possesses a very sympathetic appearance, with an aura of great distinction. His fine head – almost that of an old man – recalls the type of a handsome, benign, elderly Russian priest. His features are certainly not characteristic of German good looks, and I cannot conceive why some learned ethnographer (Brahms himself told me this after I had spoken of the impression his appearance made upon me) chose to reproduce his head on the first page of his books as being highly characteristic of German features. A certain softness of outline, pleasing curves, rather*

long and slightly grizzled hair, kind grey eyes, and a thick beard, freely sprinkled with white – all this recalled at once the type of purebred Great Russian so frequently met with among our clergy. Utterly free from vanity, Brahms's manner is very simple, his humour comfortable and jovial.

He gave a more informal account in a letter to his publisher Jürgenson:

I've been on the booze with Brahms. He is tremendously nice – not at all proud, as I'd expected, but remarkably straightforward and entirely without arrogance. He has a very cheerful disposition and I must say that the hours I spent in his company have left me with nothing but the pleasantest memories.

It was a tour of many memorable meetings: Dvořák, Gounod, Massenet, the twenty-two-year-old Ferruccio Busoni, who impressed him enormously, and at a rehearsal in Leipzig, another, older man, of unfamiliar appearance:

There entered the room a very short, middle-aged man, exceedingly fragile in appearance, with shoulders of unequal height, fair hair brushed back from his forehead, and a very slight, almost boyish, beard and moustache. There was nothing very striking about the features of this man (who immediately attracted my sympathy) for it would be impossible to call them handsome or regular, but he had an uncommon charm, and blue eyes – not large, but irresistibly fascinating – recalling the glance of a charming and candid child. I rejoiced in the depths of my heart when we were introduced to each other, and it turned out that this personality, so inexplicably attractive to me, belonged to one whose warmly emotional music had long ago won my heart. It was none other than Edvard Grieg.

Perhaps the most unexpected meeting (had it been expected it might have excited some dread) was with a lady to whom he had given hardly a thought for many years at a dinner party in Berlin given in Tchaikovsky's honour: 'Artôt was there. I was inexpressibly glad to see her again. We made friends at once, without so much as a word about the past. Her husband, Padilla, embraced me most heartily. Tomorrow she is giving a dinner. As an elderly woman [of fifty-three!] she remains just as fascinating as she was twenty years ago.'

In Berlin he heard for the first time a work by Richard Strauss, who could be glad that Tchaikovsky was not employed as a critic. 'Bülow has taken him up just now,' he wrote to Modest, 'as formerly he took up Brahms and others. To my mind such an astounding lack of talent, united to such pretentiousness, has never before existed in the history of the world.'

We have already sampled Tchaikovsky's cavalier and uninhibited dismissals of other notable composers, and on the whole his resistance to them remained unchanged throughout his life. His extravagantly negative reaction to Strauss, however, may have been influenced to some degree by the fact that in Berlin, at that time, he himself was not enjoying the success he had met with elsewhere in Germany. He was as inconsistent in his reactions to criticism as he was in most other things. It could rankle with him for years and cause him to break off friendships, or he could take it quite lightly, as when he reports from Germany: 'The newspapers have published long articles about me. They slate me a good deal, but pay me far more attention than our own press. Their views are sometimes actually quite funny. A critic speaking of the variations in the Third Suite, says that one describes a sitting of the Holy Synod and another an explosion of dynamite!'

Tchaikovsky's extravagantly negative reaction to Strauss may have been influenced by the fact that in Berlin, he himself was not enjoying the success he had met with elsewhere in Germany.

If his reception in Germany was mixed (though predominantly triumphant), his welcome in Prague was little short of sensational. Since Prague was reputed by many to be the most musical city in Europe, the accolades he received there were more than usually meaningful to him, for they increased to the point of rapture the bond with his idol, Mozart – he inaccurately believed that Prague was 'the first city to recognise the genius of Mozart'.

Since Prague was reputed by many to be the most musical city in Europe, the accolades he received there were more than usually meaningful to him.

Rather like Liszt in the Berlin of the 1830s, Tchaikovsky was treated not as a mere musician (albeit a great one) but as if he were a high potentate from a distant, rich and important land. He made an almost royal progress to all the principal places of interest. On one occasion he entered the Town Hall while the city council was in session, and the entire body of members rose as one to greet him. On another evening he was serenaded at his hotel by the famous Hlalol choral society. He listened from his balcony, watching the street fill with onlookers, and then came down to thank the singers in person. In his speech to them he promised to compose something expressly for the society, eliciting a chorus of loud cheering. On another day he was presented at the Students' Union: more cheering. In his diary he speaks of this as 'a deeply touching occasion'. Accompanied by yet more cheering, he was then led off to the public rehearsal of the concert. The evening wound up with a brilliant soirée at which he was the guest of honour. With few exceptions, life went on like this from country to country. As he modestly wrote to Mme von Meck:

> *The public give me a most enthusiastic reception. Of course, all this is very nice, but at the same time I feel so utterly exhausted I scarcely know how I shall manage to get through all that still lies ahead of me. Can you recognise in this Russian musician, touring and fêted all over Europe, the*

man who only a few years ago fled from life and society, and lived in solitude, abroad, or in the country?

Tchaikovsky in the grounds of his house at Frolovskoye

From now on, this self-styled refugee 'from life and society' would live in the public eye as never before. He was well on his way to being the most famous musician in the world.

On returning to Russia in April 1888, after four months abroad, Tchaikovsky moved out of Maidanovo and into another house, this one at Frolovskoye (the same general area). It struck him, at least for the present, as a corner of Heaven:

Ah, how pleasant, how free it is here! The sun has already set and in the broad meadow in front of the main entrance the scorching heat of the day has yielded to the cool of the evening. The air is rich with the scent of lilac and of freshly cut hay, the May bugs break the silence with their bass notes, the nightingales sing, and another song floats over from somewhere far away. Before turning in, I sit for a long time in front of the open window, breathing in the marvellous, fresh air, listening to all the sounds of a spring night, the charms of which cannot be spoilt even by the petulant croaking of the frogs.

For a while, music took second place to nature. To Modest, in May, he confessed: 'I have not yet begun to work, except at some corrections. To speak frankly, I feel as yet no impulse for creative work. What does this mean? Have I written myself out? No ideas, no inclination? Still I am hoping gradually to collect material for a symphony.'

That symphony was to be his Fifth, and his greatest to date. As he contented himself for the moment with 'collecting' material from his imagination (for this was no folk-based exercise), he complemented his pleasure in the joys of nature with a renewed immersion in the joys, and attendant reflections, of literature. A fluent linguist, he read in several languages, including Latin, wrote poetry (an enthusiasm since early childhood), and numbered some distinguished authors, including Chekhov, among his friends. Tolstoy was an admiring acquaintance whom Tchaikovsky revered above all living writers, without presuming to claim him as a friend. He was also, as we have seen, passionately fond of Dickens. Another enthusiasm was George Eliot.

Although he never fancied himself as a critic, and has been criticised himself for a lack of 'taste' in the verse he chose to set, Tchaikovsky's correspondence reveals a thoughtful and often incisive literary connoisseur. In a letter from this period to the Grand Duke Constantine, an amateur poet of some quality who had sent Tchaikovsky a volume of his verses, he reflected:

Tchaikovsky's correspondence reveals a thoughtful and often incisive literary connoisseur.

When I read Jukovsky's translation of The Odyssey, *or his* Undine, *or Gniedich's version of* The Iliad, *I suffer from the intolerable monotony of the Russian hexameter as compared with the Latin (I do not know the Greek), which has strength, beauty, and variety. I know the fault lies in the fact that we don't use the spondee, but I cannot understand why this should be. To my mind we ought to employ it. Another question that greatly occupies me is why, as compared with Russian poetry, German verse should be less severe in the matter of regular rhythm and metre. When I read Goethe I am astonished at his audacity as regards metrical feet, the caesura, etc., which he carries so far that, to the unpractised ear, many of his verses can seem scarcely like verse at all. At the same time, the ear is only taken by surprise – it is never offended. Were a Russian poet to do the same, one would be conscious of a certain lameness. Is it in consequence of the peculiar qualities of our language, or because tradition allows greater freedom to the Germans than to us? I do not know if I express myself quite correctly; I only state that, as regards regularity, refinement, and euphony, much more is expected from the Russian than from the German poet. I should be glad to find some explanation of this.*

By the end of June, he had basically completed his sketches for the Fifth Symphony. As he had anticipated, progress was difficult, and it can hardly have been eased by the fact that for some time he had been working in parallel on another major project. This was the programmatic fantasy overture *Hamlet*, of which he had completed the preliminary score by 4 July.

Roughly a week later, he made an entry in his diary that is not only fascinating and important for the biographer but intriguing in its wider implications, for if what he writes is true of letters it is equally true of great men's diaries:

It seems to me that letters are not perfectly sincere – I am judging by myself. No matter to whom I am writing, I am always

> *conscious of the effect of my letter, not only upon the person to whom it is addressed, but upon any chance reader. Consequently I embroider. I often take pains to make the tone of a letter simple and sincere – or at least to make it appear so. But apart from letters written at the moment when I am worked upon, I am never quite myself in my correspondence. These letters are to me a source of repentance, and often of agonising regret. When I read the correspondence of great men, published after their death, I am always disturbed by a vague sense of insincerity and falsehood.*

No reader or biographer, however, can doubt the sincerity of Tchaikovsky's passion for nature and the countryside. Throughout his life, it was one of the surest antidotes to his recurrent depressions, and though he tried to stick to the daily plan mapped out in Maidanovo, his new surroundings with their own internal rhythms forced a rather different pace on him, at least to begin with:

> *My life here has already settled into a steady, regular pattern. After my morning coffee I go for a walk in the garden, and when I have been right round I wander out through some little wooden gates, carry on across a ditch and then, quite soon, there opens out a garden which has run wild and has turned into a delightful, quiet, cosy little spot, with an extraordinary variety of birds. The call of the oriole and the trilling of the nightingale are the songs I find the most entrancing. In some places, the paths are so lushly overgrown, and the greenery so fresh and clean that one might be in the depths of a forest. I go for a walk here, then sit down somewhere in the shade and spend about an hour there, just being. There's nothing to compare with these moments of isolation, surrounded by greenery and flowers, when you sit listening, and observing*

> *that organic life which, though it may manifest itself silently, speaks more loudly of infinity in time and space than all the rumble of the roads and the bustle of town life. When I have been abroad, amongst all the striking and luxuriant beauties which nature provides in the south, I have never yet experienced these moments of holy rapture in the contemplation of nature, which are higher, for me, even than the delights of art. I like open places at sunset, and the meadow, in front of the house, with trees, lilac bushes, and the stream at its edge, makes an enchanting evening walk. Oh what a marvellous life this is!*

In the countryside, the little boy in Tchaikovsky, never very far away, could play and explore without constraint:

> *I have found a considerable quantity of mushrooms, which are one of my greatest pleasures in the summer. All night I dreamt of enormous, fat, red mushrooms. When I woke up it struck me that these mushroomy dreams were very childish. And indeed, when one lives alone with nature, one does develop a childlike receptivity to the simplest, most guileless joys that it offers. Yesterday, for instance, it gave me the greatest delight to spend what must have been about an hour by the path in the garden, watching how a snail got in amongst a tiny bunch of ants. Even when living entirely on one's own, I cannot understand how anyone could be bored in the country for a single moment. Surely there is more interest in that little scene, which shows in microscopic form the whole tragedy of the conflict amongst so many individuals, than in the vacuous chatter, the pathetic and pointless flapping about which is the essence of how most of society spends its time.*

César Cui, one of the 'Mighty Handful' and an implacable critic of Tchaikovsky

Further evidence that Tchaikovsky was not of that company came with the first performances, in November 1888, of *Hamlet* and the Fifth Symphony. Both were given in St Petersburg, a week apart (in each case with Tchaikovsky conducting), and both were ecstatically received by audience and orchestra alike. In addition to the cheers and bouquets at the first concert, there was a triple fanfare from the orchestra, and Tchaikovsky was publicly presented with honorary membership of the St Petersburg Philharmonic Society. Sadly, the critics were not so kind. César Cui, Tchaikovsky's long-time foe, was merciless, dismissing the symphony as 'unoriginal, characterless, routine stuff: mere sound predominating over music'. He was wrong on every count, as history, the public and conductors have demonstrated time and again ever since.

Fortunately, Tchaikovsky knew nothing of this review when he departed for Prague the day after the second concert, to conduct both the symphony and the Czech premiere of *Eugene Onegin*. By now predictably, both events met with tumultuous applause. Tchaikovsky returned home, however, in low spirits, having learned en route of the death from tuberculosis of his niece Vera Davïdova, and the suicide of a friend. Greeting him on his return was

Hamlet and the Fifth Symphony were given in St Petersburg (in each case with Tchaikovsky conducting), and both were ecstatically received.

Cui's review. As often before, and not for the last time, his response to negative comment was to crumple, and to agree with even the severest of his critics. As he wrote at the time:

> *After two performances of my new Symphony in Petersburg, and one in Prague, I have come to the conclusion that it is a failure. There is something repellent, something superfluous, patchy, and insincere, which the public instinctively recognises. It was obvious to me that the ovations I received were prompted more by my earlier work, and that the symphony itself did not really please the audience. My consciousness of this brings me a sharp twinge of self-dissatisfaction. Am I really played out, as they say? Can I merely repeat and ring the changes on my earlier idiom? Last night I looked through* our *Symphony* [No. 4]. *What a difference! How immeasurably superior it is! This is all so very, very sad!*

These searing post-criticism collapses seldom lasted for long, however, and he can only have been cheered by a letter he received at about this time from Dvořák in Prague:

> *Dear Friend,*
> *When you were lately with us here I promised to write to you on the subject of your opera* Onegin. *I am now moved to do so, not only in answer to your request, but also by my own impulse to express all I felt on hearing your work. I confess with joy that your opera made a deep impression on me – the kind I expect to receive only from a genuine work of art, and I do not hesitate to tell you that not one of your compositions has given me such pleasure as* Onegin. *It is a wonderful creation, full of glowing emotion and poetry, and finely elaborated in all its details; in short, this music*

is captivating, and penetrates our hearts so deeply that we can never forget it. Whenever I go to hear it I feel myself transported into another world. I congratulate you upon this marvellous work. God grant you may give us many another like it.

That was not to be, but he did something almost as good. The director of the Imperial Theatres approached Tchaikovsky with a commission for a new three-act ballet, **The Sleeping Beauty**. To begin with, at least, it seems to have come relatively easily. He completed the prologue and the first two acts before the end of January, and most of the third act during the course of yet another European tour, this one embracing Cologne, Frankfurt, Dresden, Berlin, Geneva, Paris and London. By the time he returned home, all that remained to be done was the orchestration.

The director of the Imperial Theatres approached Tchaikovsky with a commission for a new three-act ballet, *The Sleeping Beauty*.

Ironically, given its start, the finished product was a long time coming. Unlike the bulk of the original composition, and somewhat to Tchaikovsky's surprise, the orchestration proved far more difficult, and gave him a great deal of trouble. It kept him well occupied throughout a summer described by Modest as one of 'peaceful monotony', given over mainly to composition but occasionally leavened by little parties at home – which on the whole he enjoyed. Particularly memorable to Modest was his brother's reaction to the three-year-old daughter of Alexey Legoshin – a friend of Tchaikovsky's. He was, Modest writes, 'altogether fascinated by her prettiness, her clear, bell-like voice, her charming ways, and clever little head. He would spend hours romping with the child, listening to her chatter, even acting as her nursemaid.' Unlike many confirmed bachelors, he had a great love of children and was able to entertain them almost as though he himself had returned to their age.

As was now becoming usual following the completion of a major work, Tchaikovsky left Russia almost immediately after the ballet's premiere. He headed again for Italy, where in Florence he set to work at once on a new stage work, an opera based on Pushkin's dark, even ghoulish, story **The Queen of Spades**. This was as quick in coming as *The Sleeping Beauty* had been slow. Within six weeks it was fully sketched, and six weeks after that it was finished. It was characteristic of Tchaikovsky's emotional involvement with his characters that he was often in tears while composing the tragic last scene. Also typical was the decision to follow the opera with a work that in almost every respect is its exact opposite: the elegant, undemanding, charmingly sophisticated *Souvenir de Florence* (see page 106).

His most substantial souvenir of Florence, however, was *The Queen of Spades*, which, exceptionally among his operas, was a hit from the start.

Interlude V:
Tchaikovsky in Song

Outside Russia, Tchaikovsky's songs are perhaps the most neglected branch of his output, and are therefore largely unknown. A handful have become moderately popular, but even the most famous of these, a Russian translation of Goethe and best known in English as 'None but the Lonely Heart', is hardly on the lips of most music lovers today. The reasons for this degree of neglect are easier to explain than to justify. Central Europe is the home of the 'art' song; the literature is dominated by an overwhelming treasury of masterpieces by Schubert, Schumann, Brahms and Wolf, who between them brought the medium to its highest peak of perfection and explored through it virtually every state of mind and feeling. By contrast, England, which was widely known in nineteenth-century Germany as 'das Land ohne Musik' ('the land without music'), was home to the Victorian after-dinner ballad, an altogether less exalted breed. Before Mikhail Glinka in the 1830s, there was no tradition of Russian art song at all; the idea of any home-produced Russian art music began with him. By the time Tchaikovsky came of age, the Russian art song did exist but was often closer in quality and expressive character to the Victorian ballad than to the German Lied, despite the seminal influence of Schumann. This type of Russian song was known as a 'romance'. To many non-Russians, the image of Tchaikovsky's songs (based almost entirely on hearsay) is of a sea of superficial pap. Closer acquaintance reveals an archipelago of exceptions, but the sea remains expansive. It is not the aim of this section to deal primarily in value judgements and opinions, informed or otherwise, but to set Tchaikovsky's songs in context and to explore some of his attitudes and techniques.

Neither as a composer nor as a man can Tchaikovsky be altogether absolved from a charge of sentimentality. To a certain extent he was born to it: it was almost a family tradition, engendered and perpetuated not by his mother, who was notably reserved, but by his father, whose verbal excesses were legendary.

Reactions to music will always be primarily subjective, and the critical attribution of moral or emotional hypocrisy to a composer on the basis of his music alone is a dangerous and presumptuous game, if a frequently practised one. Even some respected musicologists and biographers are apt to dismiss Tchaikovsky's most famous song as the height (or implicitly, the depth) of sentimentality – not so much excessive as insincere in its emotion. However, other equally authoritative commentators praise it lavishly. It must always be for the listener to decide. Ultimately, of course, the moods or motives of the composer are irrelevant, for the music itself is all that matters. Even so, the attribution to Tchaikovsky of insincerity as a composer, while generally undeserved, is implicitly supported by the man himself when he writes that his last symphony 'is far and away the most *sincere* of all my works'. It therefore remains a fact that for many commentators Tchaikovsky's songs are predominantly sentimental, or melodramatic (or bland to the point of offence), and that they seldom even hint

It remains a fact that for many commentators Tchaikovsky's songs are predominantly sentimental, or melodramatic (or bland to the point of offence).

at what he might have been able to achieve in this medium. But standpoints of any kind aside, there is no doubt that when it comes to the fullest appreciation of this repertoire it is evidently a great advantage to be Russian.

Tchaikovsky's approach to the writing of songs was distinctly his own. He was not rigid about it, and in fact he explored a wide variety of song types and made some interesting experiments; but his priorities were always musical, and if this meant tinkering with the verses he had chosen to set, then so be it. Thus we find him not only repeating words and phrases but changing the order of lines and even adding extra words.

Such an outwardly cavalier attitude to other men's work was hardly peculiar to the Romantic era, let alone to Tchaikovsky. At this time, the liberties taken by performers with a composer's text were often colossal; but while wholly unobjectionable to most listeners it greatly incensed certain musicians, most notably Tchaikovsky's bad fairy, César Cui. In a bitter attack he levelled a number of substantial charges that were not to be shrugged off lightly:

> *[Tchaikovsky's] talent does not possess the flexibility required for real vocal music . . . He did not acknowledge the equal rights of poetry and music. He regarded the text with despotic presumption... Having chosen texts with no artistic value, Tchaikovsky treated them without ceremony. In the music, the punctuation is very badly observed. Tchaikovsky could not be concise or laconic; he did not know how to write briefly . . . Never particular in the choice of musical ideas, he nevertheless let go of them with difficulty and developed them in every possible way. But more often than not, this development consists of repetition and variation, effected with the skilful craft of the experienced technician.*

Tchaikovsky did not shrug, lightly or otherwise. He faced the charges head-on and with considerable clarity and force:

> *Our musical critics, often losing sight of the fact that the essential in vocal music is truthful reproduction of emotion and state of mind, look primarily for defective accentuations and for all kinds of small declamatory oversights in general. They collect them maliciously and reproach the composer with an assiduousness worthy of a better cause. In this Cui has especially distinguished himself and has gone on doing so on every occasion up to now . . . Absolute accuracy of musical declamation is a negative quality, and its importance should not be exaggerated. What does the repetition of words, even of whole sentences, matter? There are cases where such repetitions are completely natural and in harmony with reality. Under the influence of strong emotion a person repeats one and the same exclamation and sentence very often. I do not find anything out of accordance with the truth when an old, dull-witted governess [in* The Queen of Spades*] repeats her eternal refrain about decency at every appropriate opportunity during her long admonition. But even if that never happened in real life, I should feel no embarrassment in impudently turning my back on 'real' truth in favour of 'artistic' truth. The two are completely different . . . For people to confuse them when contrasting speech and song is simply dishonest.*

This distinction between 'real' and 'artistic' truth was central to Tchaikovsky's compositional credo. Though he was by no means insensitive to language (whether poetry or prose, he drew on it for inspiration), he used it as a springboard to musical representation – emotional, psychological,

The distinction between 'real' and 'artistic' truth was central to Tchaikovsky's compositional credo.

'pictorial', vocal and physical – and as a vehicle for self-expression. He was loath to let verbal language subvert the demands, as he saw them, of musical form.

On the specific matter of word repetition, Cui and others were overreacting with a vengeance. Word repetition has been a staple of musical settings for many centuries, both in folk and art traditions. Take 'Mary had a little lamb, little lamb, little lamb, / Mary had a little lamb, its fleece was white as snow', for instance – and there are innumerable similar examples in opera and oratorio. Musical form itself, perhaps uniquely among the arts, is dependent on repetition and often founded precisely on that basis. Standard 'ternary' form – the normal structure of the operatic 'da capo' aria and of common-or-garden sonata form – is universally represented as A–B–A, where A is the basic material, B is a contrasting middle section (often developing material from A), and the second appearance of A is basically a repeat (often literal) of its first appearance.

Indeed, the repetitious nature of musical organisation is such that the following illustrative expansion of a verse by Thomas Love Peacock is only the most modest analogy with the sort of thing we take for granted in music (the original, incidentally, contains no repetition of any kind):

The poor man's sins, the poor man's sins,
are glaring, glaring, glaring;
the poor man's sins, they glare, they glare
in the face of ghostly warning;
in the face, in the face, in the face, in the face;
in the face of ghostly warning.
He is caught in the fact,
he is caught in the fact,
he is caught in the fact,

of an overt act,
he is caught in the fact,
of an overt act –
buying greens on a Sunday morning.

We should remember, too, (as Tchaikovsky never forgot) that verse – and sung verse most of all – is already a form of ritualised speech. There was no need for him to cite reality in his own defence.

Like Mozart, Tchaikovsky thoroughly understood the human voice. He loved it, and he wrote for it lovingly. His songs suit music and singers equally well. But for Tchaikovsky, the music, not the singer, came first. He conceived most of his songs as well-balanced structures, easily translatable into instrumental terms – witness the widespread success of some of them in transcriptions for violin and for other instruments. The songs, as structures, are usually 'framed' between a formal piano prelude and a corresponding (often identical) postlude, which seldom do much to enhance the essence of the music in between. This has been criticised particularly in songs like *If Only I Had Known*, one of the better ones, whose extended introduction (duly repeated at the end) admittedly contains important thematic elements but seems otherwise to have little or nothing to do with the substance of the song itself. Here, writ large, is proof that when Tchaikovsky didn't cover up the seams, which was often the case, it was not because he was incapable but because, for one reason or another, he did not care to. Taken as a whole, his songs are an irrefutable demonstration of his competence. But while he was a practical musician, whose habits intentionally precluded waiting around for inspiration, he was also subject to periods of laziness and cynicism. He could churn out

For Tchaikovsky, the music, not the singer, came first.

reams of potboilers (mainly piano pieces and songs), fully aware that his reputation would survive such note-spinning – even as the kopeks from these potboilers tumbled in.

Tchaikovsky was a born melodist, with a natural if not generally very adventurous sense of harmony and a great facility for improvisation. He soon developed a repertoire of more or less stock gestures that could be easily recycled in numerous combinations: harmonic progressions that turn up in various guises and circumstances, particular ways of spicing up otherwise humdrum chords, weaving in little decorative patterns, anchoring everything to a descending scale in the bass, etc. For all his self-doubts Tchaikovsky was a great composer (and he knew it), but he was also a born hack, and as long as he could function as the former, he was relatively unabashed about being the latter. He was also aware that many among his audience – and more to the point, many of the people who actually bought his music – were unable to tell the difference. At either end of the spectrum, he was a canny professional, a craftsman who knew his business, and how to go about it. A case in point, particularly where his songs are concerned, was his talent for plotting and placing the optimally effective climax.

For all his self-doubts Tchaikovsky was a great composer (and he knew it), but he was also a born hack. At either end of the spectrum, he was a canny professional, a craftsman who knew his business, and how to go about it.

Any composer, but particularly a great one, is at one level a calculating emotional manipulator, who plays with his listeners as much as he plays with his notes. There is evidence that in composing his songs Tchaikovsky would sometimes begin by isolating the point in the text where the musical climax should occur, and, more interestingly still, would compose the climax first, before attending to the rest of the song. This is all of a piece with Rimsky-Korsakov's account of the procedures adopted by Balakirev and 'The Five', as quoted on page 199. It also stands in a fascinating relationship to Rachmaninov's obsession with every piece being focused on a particular, culminating climax, towards which all before it leads, and from which all that follows flows. This is a deeply Russian trait.

Equally intriguing, in Tchaikovsky's case, is a sketch – for **To Forget so Soon**, composed in 1870 to words by Apukhtin – where we find him composing the 'accompaniment' before devising the melody above it (this is sketched out only at the end). The fact is that in many of his best songs, the real essence of the music is to be found in the piano part (perhaps one should avoid the term 'accompaniment'). A striking case in point, and one of his most boldly experimental adventures, is 'New Greek Song', subtitled 'In Dark Hell', the last of the *Six Romances*, Op. 16 from 1872. In this setting of one of Apollon Maykov's *New Greek Songs*, the voice does not always have the main tune but often appears as a counter-melody in the overall texture. This idea of a continuous melody passing frequently from voice to accompaniment and then back again, in an unbroken chain of melodic variations, shows us Tchaikovsky at his most original and resourceful. There is no sign of the hack in any part of this amazing song, which (like its inspiration, Liszt's *Totentanz*) is a series of variations on the grim medieval plainchant 'Dies irae'. Just as strong, however, are the parallels with two other of Liszt's works: the 'Dante Sonata', which also depicts the Inferno (though not exclusively, as here), and the first *Mephisto Waltz*. Further quotations include the Protestant chorale 'Weinen, Klagen, Zorgen, Zagen', which was famously used by Bach and revived by Liszt, and which forms the basis for much of this song (no accident, it being likewise concerned with tears and the sufferings of humanity). The four-part writing in this quite remarkable work – three parts for the piano, one for the singer – is impeccable. And the words are

A continuous melody passing frequently from voice to accompaniment and then back again shows us Tchaikovsky at his most original and resourceful.

expressed and supplemented by the music so well that even Cui acknowledged the song as flawless.

It has often been said that many of Tchaikovsky's songs are too operatic by half, too far removed in style, projection and attitude from the relative intimacy of the middle-class drawing room for which they were intended. But in this he was a child of his time. The distinction between 'aria' and 'romance' was often fuzzy in nineteenth-century Russia but, even so, we have here another classic case of Tchaikovsky being pulled in two directions at once. There is on the one hand the well-behaved, conservatoire-trained, 'westernised' composer, with all his concern for balance, classical form and theoretical decorum, and on the other a profoundly, even extravagantly emotional artist whose desire to ravish the world with timeless melodies and seismic passions easily led him to excess. But if drama sometimes spilled over into melodrama, as some feel it does in songs like 'Don Juan's Serenade' (a Tolstoy setting, whose title is already loaded with operatic associations), it can be melodrama of a very high order, as indeed it is in this song. In closing, it should be added that the 'operatic' character attributed to many of Tchaikovsky's songs is often not intrinsic but the fault of singers, who habitually or traditionally mistake them for arias.

Tchaikovsky's desire to ravish the world with timeless melodies and seismic passions easily led him to excess.

Chapter 6

The New Statesman: At Home and Abroad 1888–1891

The New Statesman: At Home and Abroad 1888–1891

When he began his next important work, in the autumn of 1890, Tchaikovsky had little inkling of the emotional bombshell that was about to explode inside him. On 6 October, while staying with Anatoly in Tiflis, he received a letter from Mme von Meck, announcing that she had in fact gone bankrupt and that Tchaikovsky's allowance was therefore at an end. He was thunderstruck, not because of

The Tchaikovsky brothers, 1890: (left to right) Anatoly, Nikolay, Ippolit, Pyotr and Modest

the money but because of the letter's implications. His first response (to her at any rate) was nevertheless sympathetic, concerned and generous:

> *My very dear friend!*
> *Your news profoundly grieved me, not for myself at all, but for you. Those are no empty words. It would, of course, be untrue to say that such a drop in my income will have no effect on my material prosperity, but it will not affect me as much as you may suspect. The point is that my income has increased substantially in recent years and there is no reason to suppose that it will not go on doing so, at an ever more rapid rate. So if I am accountable for any fraction of your endless cares and anxieties, I beg you, for God's sake, to understand with absolute certainty that I can contemplate this pecuniary loss without a trace of bitterness. Believe me, that this is the simple truth. You know I am no striker of poses, no master of the empty phrase. What really matters is that you, with your very grand life style, are the one who will suffer deprivations. This is terribly hard and vexatious to bear . . .*
>
> *I have to confess that I was hurt by your final words* ['Do not forget, and think of me sometimes'] *but I cannot think that you meant them seriously. Can you really believe that my thoughts of you have been dependent on my receiving money from you? How could I forget for a single moment all that you have done for me, and the depth of the gratitude I owe you? I can say without exaggeration that you saved my life. But for your friendship, your sympathy and your material assistance, I should certainly have gone out of my mind and come to an untimely end. But you enabled me once again to rally my forces and to take up once more my chosen vocation. Rest assured, dear friend, that I shall remember and bless you to the end of*

my days and with my last breath. I am glad that now that you can no longer spend your riches on me, I can at last tell you with all the force at my disposal of my unbounded and passionate gratitude – except that it is quite impossible to put it into words. You yourself cannot understand the full extent of what you have done for me, or you would never have suggested that now you are poor, I should only think of you sometimes!!! I can say with all the honesty of my heart I have never forgotten you and never will forget you even for a single moment, because when I think about myself my thoughts always and inevitably turn directly to you.

I kiss your hand with all my heart's warmth, and implore you to believe, once and for all, that no one can feel more keenly for your trouble than do I.

Yours

P. Tchaikovsky

. . . Forgive this badly written letter, but I am too much upset to write legibly.

What most painfully wounded Tchaikovsky was not so much the end of his allowance as the fact that Mme von Meck was quite clearly terminating their correspondence, and hence their friendship, at the same time. She was ill and weak, and, as he knew, had lost the use of one hand; but the reasons she gave for ending his annuity were demonstrably false. Her financial problems were both slight and temporary, which she recognised, and she remained a very rich woman indeed. That was not the essence of Tchaikovsky's distress, however, as a far less noble letter to his publisher demonstrates:

Mme von Meck was quite clearly terminating their correspondence, the reasons she gave for ending his annuity were demonstrably false.

The fact is that I am *offended – deeply, deeply, deeply offended. When I was receiving her generous donations,*

> *I never felt embarrassment. Now, in retrospect, I do. My pride has been wounded. My faith in her, my belief in her unlimited generosity, in her willingness to make any sacrifice for me, has been betrayed. To tell the truth, what I would like now is for her to be so decisively ruined that she would need my help. The entire affair has turned out to be nothing but a stupid and sordid joke, which I find sickening and shameful.*

Nevertheless, he did try to resuscitate the correspondence, if only through third parties, but the result was a deafening silence. Among the third parties was Mme von Meck's son-in-law, the violinist Władysław Pachulski, who received the following from the estranged composer:

> *I know that Nadezhda Filaretovna is ill, and weak, and that her nerves are upset, so that she can no longer write to me as before. And not for the world would I add to her sufferings. But what grieves, bewilders, and I must say deeply hurts me is that she has ceased to feel any interest in me. Even if she no longer desired me to go on corresponding directly with her, it could have been easily arranged for you and Yuliya Karlovna [von Meck's daughter] to have acted as links between us. But she has never once made even the slightest enquiry through either of you as to how I am living, or what I am doing. I have endeavoured, through you, to re-establish my correspondence with N.F., but not one of your letters has contained more than a courteous reference to my efforts.*
>
> *You are doubtless aware that last September she informed me that she could no longer pay my annuity. You must also know how I replied to her. I wished and hoped that our relations might remain unchanged. But unhappily this seemed impossible, because of her total estrangement from me. The*

result has been that all contact between us was brought to an end the moment I ceased to receive her money. This situation lowers me in my own estimation; it makes the remembrance of the money I accepted from her well-nigh intolerable; it worries and weighs upon me more than I can say. When I was in the country last autumn I reread all of N.F.'s earlier letters to me. No illness, no misfortune, no financial anxieties could ever – so it seemed to me – change the feelings she expresses there. And yet they have changed. Perhaps I idealised N.F. because I did not know her personally. I could not conceive change in such a demigoddess. I would sooner have believed that the earth could open up beneath me than that our relations could suffer change. But the inconceivable has happened, and all my ideas of human nature, all my faith in the best of mankind, have been turned upside down. My peace is broken, and the share of happiness fate has allotted me is embittered and spoilt.

No doubt Nadezhda Filaretovna has dealt me this cruel blow unconsciously and unintentionally. But never in my life have I felt so lowered, or had my pride so profoundly injured, as in this matter. The worst is that, on account of her shattered health, I dare not show her all the troubles of my heart, lest I should grieve or upset her. I may not speak out, which alone would be my sole relief. However, let this suffice. Even as it is, I may regret having said all this – but I felt the need of giving vent to some of my bitterness. Of course, I do not wish a word to be said to N.F.

Should she ever inquire about me, tell her that I have settled down to work in Maidanovo. You may add that I am well.

It was his last attempt. Mme von Meck maintained her silence until Tchaikovsky's death, and followed him two months later.

For whatever reason – and it is likely to be sheer coincidence – Tchaikovsky's career went from strength to strength after he received Mme von Meck's final letter. Revered and adored in every country where European music was heard, accorded what today would be called pop-idol status wherever he conducted, he should by rights have felt on top of the world. But Mme von Meck had blown a hole in his life too big to heal. In the words of Modest, her silence occasioned 'a secret anguish that darkened his life to the end of his days'. She was not, however, as some had feared, the Muse without whom he could no longer compose. In that role, her successor was already well in place:

Revered and adored in every country where European music was heard, accorded what today would be called pop-idol status, Tchaikovsky should by rights have felt on top of the world.

My darling Bob,
When I am abroad, I suffer the most terrible, inexpressible, maddeningly agonising homesickness. But most of all, of course, I think of you, and long to see you, and to hear your voice. I feel sometimes that I would give up ten years of my life (and as you know, I value my life very much), if you could appear before me even for a second. Oh Bob, I do adore you so! And you remember that I told you that even greater than my joy at beholding you with my own eyes is my suffering when I am without you!

'Darling Bob' was Tchaikovsky's young nephew Vladimir Davïdov. The boy had been the apple of Tchaikovsky's eye since his early childhood, and as he entered his teens he was fast becoming the single greatest source of pleasure and consolation in Tchaikovsky's day-to-day life. In 1884, when Bob was thirteen, Tchaikovsky, then forty-four, wrote to Modest in ebullient mood: 'Ah! Our friendship is terrific! And do you know, for the first time he displays a strong liking for me. Formerly he only allowed himself to be adored, while now he seems to have begun to value my adoration. And truly, I do adore him – and the longer, the more powerfully. What a delightful specimen of humankind he is!'

It is in Tchaikovsky's diaries, however, rather than his correspondence, that we learn the full extent of his adoration: 'Before supper played piano duets with my darling, incomparable, wonderful, ideal Bob! In the end he will simply drive me mad with his indescribable charm . . . As soon as I am not working, I start longing for Bob and missing him. I do love him terribly. O Lord I do!'

Fully eight years later, Tchaikovsky's love for his nephew, aged twenty-one, had become something like an obsession. All of which must have been hard-going for Bob, who did not reciprocate Tchaikovsky's feelings – something which Tchaikovsky failed to grasp properly until the last year of his life.

In December of 1890, *The Queen of Spades* was first produced in St Petersburg and scored a tremendous success, leading quickly to a double commission from the Imperial Theatre for a ballet and a one-act opera.

Before he could complete either, Tchaikovsky crossed the Atlantic for the first time to make his conducting debut in the United States, followed by a brief tour which took him to New York, Philadelphia and Baltimore, and included trips to Washington DC and, most unforgettably, to the Niagara Falls. His state of mind as he set off was low even by his standards, and was deepened further by the death of his sister Alexandra (Bob's mother), news of which he saw on the last page of a newspaper on the very brink of his departure.

Tchaikovsky crossed the Atlantic for a brief tour which took him to New York, Philadelphia and Baltimore.

Tchaikovsky with Nikolay and Medea Figner, who created the roles of Hermann and Liza in The Queen of Spades, *1890*

I dashed out of the room as if stung by a hornet. After tramping through the streets with no sense of the time, I called in to see Sophie Menter and Vasya Sapelnikov. To my great good fortune, they were home, and it was there that I spent the night. My first thought was to forget about America and adjourn at once to Petersburg, but before long I realised how pointless that would have been. My sufferings, though, are truly terrible. I fear dreadfully for Bob, consoled only by the knowledge that at his age such things are weathered more easily than in later life.

The New World surpassed his highest expectations.

After a crossing that cured him of the idea that he was immune to seasickness, he arrived in the New World, which surpassed his highest expectations:

*New York, American customs, American hospitality, the look of the city, the extraordinary comfort of my accommodation – all this is very much to my taste. If I were younger I would doubtless be loving my stay in this fascinating new country. But I am enduring it – as though it were a form of punishment that the agreeable circumstances make more bearable. My thoughts and desires are one and the same: home, home, home!!! People here could not be friendlier or more considerate. They honour me, they entertain me. I seem to be ten times better known here than in Europe. When they first assured me of this, I thought it was typical American exaggeration, but it turns out to be the case. There are some pieces of mine that are still not known even in Moscow (*Hamlet*, for instance); here they play them several times a season and write whole articles and commentaries about them. They have played the Fifth Symphony two years running. Isn't this funny!!!*

At the rehearsals the players gave me a tremendously enthusiastic reception. And they played magnificently.

At that time, America's best orchestras were heavily populated by Europeans, but Tchaikovsky was no less impressed by those born in America:

The amazing generosity of these Americans has impressed me very deeply. Their life, their customs, their ways – I find all this extraordinarily interesting and new; and at every turn one comes upon things which are simply staggering in their colossal dimensions, certainly compared to anything in Europe. The place is positively bubbling over with life, and though their consuming interest is profit, the Americans are highly attentive to art. Take, for example, the vast hall whose opening was the reason for my being invited here. This building cost millions and it was paid for by music lovers. These wealthy enthusiasts maintain a permanent orchestra. We have nothing like this at home! I must admit that I find the scale and impressiveness of everything the Americans undertake tremendously attractive. I also like the comfort over which they take such pains. My room, just like every other room in all the hotels, has gas, electric light, a private bathroom and lavatory, heaps of extremely comfortable furniture, an apparatus for speaking to the reception desk and all sorts of things to make one comfortable, which don't exist at all in Europe. In short, there is a great deal about this country that I like enormously and find profoundly interesting.

'I must admit that I find the scale and impressiveness of everything the Americans undertake tremendously attractive.'

As so often, however, he found the price of celebrity too high for comfort, and his old misanthropic side surfaced as expected:

> *My only pleasant hours, or rather minutes, are when I am by myself in my room in the evening and have the prospect of a night and morning without visits. The rest of the time, I feel continuously tired, as if I had just walked about twenty-five miles. I am told this is the effect of the spring air over here. Secondly, I am suffering more than ever from the company of strangers, and all the more so because I have to speak in foreign languages!*

Yet even he had to admit that there were some unexpectedly pleasant times too:

> *I spent the whole of yesterday at the house of the local music publisher, Schirmer. It was hard going at first, but towards evening, when there was a gathering of wonderfully kind and affectionate people, I suddenly felt relaxed and happy again. In general, I cannot praise the people here enough, and their friendliness towards me is extraordinary. They are even too kind, and it's too difficult for me arrange an hour to myself. But I like New York more and more. Incidentally, Central Park is quite magnificent. It's amazing to think that there are people of my generation who remember very well when it was nothing but cows grazing in fields. I have rehearsals almost every day, but on 28 May I am going to visit the Niagara Falls, and on the Third I shall be conducting in Philadelphia; on the Sixth in Baltimore and on the Ninth – at last! – I depart for home! The weather is marvellous, but too hot. And of course all the trees have come out long since.*

Among the American institutions he found difficult to enjoy, however, was the New York press:

> *'Tchaikovsky is a tall, gray, well built, interesting man, well on to sixty [!]. He seems a trifle embarrassed, and responds to the applause by a succession of brusque and jerky bows. But as soon as he grasps the baton his self-confidence returns.' That's what I read this morning in the* New York Herald. *It annoys me when they write about me personally and not just about the music. I cannot bear it when they remark on my embarrassment and are surprised at my 'short, sharp' bows.*

'Tchaikovsky conducts with the authoritative strength of a master and the band obeys his lead as one man.'

More bearable was the verdict of the same article a little further on: 'There is no sign of nervousness about him as he taps for silence. He conducts with the authoritative strength of a master and the band obeys his lead as one man.'

The next day was his birthday. And although the paper's description of him as being 'well on to sixty' was wide of the mark by almost a decade, it was an understandable mistake. As Nikolay Kashkin observed:

> *In his later years, Pyotr Il'yich aged quite drastically; his thin hair turned completely white, his face became wrinkled, and he began losing his teeth, which he found particularly depressing since it sometimes interfered with the clarity of his speech. Still more noticeable was the gradual weakening of his eyesight, which made reading in the evenings difficult, thus depriving him of his chief diversion within the creative life he pursued in the country.*

Now, however, he was not in the country, and not at home. Nor was it one of his happier birthdays:

Today I am fifty-one. And just at this moment I am feeling terribly agitated. There's a concert at two o'clock with the Third Suite. This peculiar feeling is an astonishing thing. How many times have I conducted this selfsame suite? It goes perfectly well; what is there to be frightened of? Yet I suffer intolerably. I don't think I have ever been in such a panic. Is it because they pay attention to my appearance here and my shyness makes itself apparent?

Tchaikovsky was treated like visiting royalty.

It was not. The only rational explanation of stage fright is fear of criticism, of being disapproved of, of being exposed. Had it been possible or acceptable to lower a curtain between Tchaikovsky and the audience, the chances are that his nerves would have been dramatically diminished, if not banished altogether. In any case, the concert was an outstanding success and Tchaikovsky was treated like visiting royalty.

Once again, I was given a supper reception and created, as they say in today's papers, 'a sensation'. It's very hard to find time for writing letters. When I have a spare minute in the morning I write my diary. Today my New York chapter comes to an end. And the press, throughout, have sung my praises to an extent I never would have dreamt of in Russia. In the intervals and after the concert the ladies would gather together in a great crowd to look at me, and some of them would come up and express their enthusiasm to me. They have all been terribly kind to me. Indeed the time is now beginning to pass quickly and in a mere ten days I hope to be departing for home. Today and tomorrow will be difficult, in that I won't have a minute of freedom: but on the other hand on Monday I go unaccompanied to Niagara. After that I have to go to so many towns, one after the other, that I hope my day of departure will creep up unnoticed.

Wherever he went, his reception was the same: 'I am besieged by visitors: reporters, composers, librettists, and, above all, absolute mountains of letters from all corners of America asking for my autograph. To all of which I conscientiously reply.'

'I am besieged by absolute mountains of letters from all corners of America asking for my autograph. To all of which I conscientiously reply.'

Among the apparently endless stream of visitors were two Russian ladies – the first compatriots he had encountered since his arrival. His reaction was unexpectedly intense: 'Since this was my first chance to have a heart-to-heart talk in Russian, there was a scene: tears sprang suddenly to my eyes, my voice quavered, and I burst out in uncontrollable sobbing. I rushed into another room and did not emerge for some time. I burn with shame when I think about this surprising episode.' But it was not to recur.

The standard of musical journalism in America was not what he was accustomed to in Europe and Russia, and he can hardly have been other than bemused by an article that appeared in *The Musical Courier*. To be fair, it was not representative of the best, but it could not have appeared in any other country:

In Tchaikovsky one finds a cultured man of the world, excessively modest and retiring. We have entertained a musical god during the past week and I fear me greatly that many of us were not aware of the fact. I bethought me, as I looked on his earnest face and heavy brow, with its condensed look about the eyes, that there stood a man who might be called the greatest in the country. Do you notice I don't say the greatest musician but the greatest man?

Let me see; of individualities living among us we still

have dear old Walt Whitman, who represents a primal force, but in the best of whose work, despite its rugged sincerity, there is always an unfinished quality . . . We have a few strong painters, fewer sculptors, our poets are mainly imitative or echoes; in a word, where in art, music, literature, politics, or religion is just such a forceful, fiery, magnetic man as Peter Tchaikovsky? You can't name him.

This man epitomizes young Russia in his music, he preaches more treason in his music than Alexander Pushkin ever uttered. He is not as profound as Brahms, but he is more poetic. Above all he paints better than the Hamburg composer. His brush is dipped into more glowing colors, his palette contains more hues and the barbaric swing of his work is tempered by European culture and restraint. Take the piano concertos in B-flat minor and G-minor. They are about as unorthodox as we can well imagine. I like the second better, but in neither of them do I find real writing for the instrument. Tchaikovsky thinks orchestral, and if the idea does not suit the keyboard well, all the worse for the keyboard.

There was a story afloat that Nicholas Rubinstein helped him to fix up the piano part of the two concertos. From Tchaikovsky I indirectly got the true story. When Peter (Pete, to be a little familiar – I don't like his middle name at all, do you?) had finished the first work he showed it to Nick Rubinstein, whom he pronounced to have been a better pianist than his brother Tony. They all lived in the same house in Moscow, Rafael Joseffy occupying the top floor, and he says that whenever he wanted to practice, Tchaikovsky always wanted to sleep, so that trouble ensued daily.

Of the multitude of celebrities Tchaikovsky met in America, none made quite such an impression as Andrew Carnegie.

Of the multitude of celebrities, political bigwigs and captains of industry whom Tchaikovsky met in America, none made quite such an impression as Andrew Carnegie, whose money helped to build the now famous concert hall named after him, the very hall Tchaikovsky was there to open. Carnegie was, as Tchaikovsky described him:

> *. . . an amazing eccentric, who from being a telegraph boy, was transformed with the passing of the years into one of America's richest men. But he has remained a simple, modest man who does not at all turn his nose up at anyone. He inspired in me an unusual warmth of feeling. Throughout the whole evening he displayed his liking for me in a remarkably individual way. He grasped me by the hand, crying out that I was uncrowned, but the most genuine king of music, he embraced me (without kissing: here men never kiss each other), and in describing my greatness, he stood on tiptoe and raised his arms above his head, finally delighting the whole company by imitating me conducting. He did this so seriously and so well, so like me, indeed, that I myself was delighted. His wife, a remarkably simple and sweet young woman, also expressed her kindly feelings towards me in a hundred different ways. All this was very gratifying for me, but at the same time, it made me feel slightly ashamed.*

The day after his dinner with Carnegie, Tchaikovsky set off, in a state of high excitement, for Niagara and its awe-inspiring falls. Part of his excitement was the prospect of seeing (and hearing) the falls themselves. Part, too, was the fact that for the first time since his arrival in America he was by himself.

> *I boarded the train in the drawing room car, which resembles our Pullman car, only the easy chairs are placed closer to one another and have their backs to the windows, but in such a way that you can comfortably turn in all*

directions. The windows are large and the view on both sides is completely unobstructed. Next to this car was the dining car, while several cars away was the smoking car, with a buffet. The connection from car to car is far more convenient than with us, since all the passageways are covered. The employees, i.e. the conductors, the waiters in the dining car and in the buffet in the smoking car, are Negroes who are all very obliging and polite. At noon I lunched (the price of the lunch is one dollar) from a menu giving one any choice of food from among all of the dishes indicated. I had supper at six, and again in exactly the same way: from a score or two dishes I could select whatever and as much as I liked, and again for a dollar. The cars are much more luxurious than ours, though there is only one class. The luxuries are entirely superfluous – even, for example, the frescoes, the crystal ornamentations, etc. There are numerous dressing rooms, i.e. compartments, in which are washstands with hot and cold water, cakes of soap, brushes, etc., and, of course, towels (of which, there is an astonishing supply here in general). You can roam about the train and wash as much as you like. There is a bath and a barber's shop. All this is convenient and comfortable – yet in spite of all this, I find our cars at home more attractive, I don't know why. Probably this is a reflection of my longing for home, which oppressed and gnawed at me madly again all day yesterday. We arrived in Buffalo at eight-thirty. Here two gentlemen were waiting for me whom Mayer asked to show me from one train to the other, as it is rather difficult to orientate oneself in the labyrinths of this junction of various lines. One of them is a Polish pianist. The meeting with these gentlemen lasted only about ten minutes. Fifty minutes after leaving Buffalo, I was in Niagara Falls.

But after his journey, he was in no mood to explore it immediately. 'I felt exceptionally weary, probably because it was so stuffy in the train, since Americans, and especially American women, are deathly afraid of drafts, as a result of which the windows are closed all the time, so there's no passage for the outside air.' No such complaint could be made about the hotel at which he was staying, though, and the next morning he awoke refreshed and eager, and shortly after breakfast set out to see the wonders of the falls at first hand:

> *The beauty and the grandeur of this sight are truly amazing. After we had visited and had a good look at the main Falls, which is more or less divided into several separate falls, some of which are colossal (the second especially), we set off to skirt round the island towards the Three Sisters Islands. This whole walk is delightful, particularly at this time of year. The greenery is absolutely fresh, and dandelions (my darlings) are blooming amongst the grass. I had a terrible urge to pick some of them, on smelling their freshness, but at every step you see notices reminding you that you're not even allowed to pick wildflowers. Then I looked at the main waterfall, Horse Shoe Fall. This is an absolutely awe-inspiring sight, which renders one quite speechless.*

Following his return to New York, he had two more conducting engagements, one in Philadelphia, the other in Baltimore, and then on 9 June he finally began the long journey home.

Interlude VI: Tchaikovsky and Russianness

Tchaikovsky was deeply imbued with Russianness; he could have stepped right out of a Russian novel.

Musically, psychologically, emotionally, intellectually, Tchaikovsky was deeply imbued with Russianness, almost from the moment of his birth. In the contradictory nature of his character, in the depth of his national identity (speaking very generally, there is no one more homesick than a homesick Russian), in his emotional volatility, his intensity, his propensity to depression, to sensuality and to alcohol (though he could drink like a champion, he seldom appeared drunk and was never an alcoholic), in his sheer theatricality, he could have stepped right out of a Russian novel. He felt his Russianness very keenly, both at home and (especially) abroad. The evidence in his music alone is irrefutable. Yet at the time, he was in one very significant respect uniquely un-Russian: he was a great, academically trained, professional composer.

When he arrived in Moscow in January 1866, set on devoting his life entirely to composition, he was one of the first Russians ever to do so. It was a brave move, both economically and socially. To the great majority of the Russian aristocracy, and much of the upper middle class to which he belonged, music was no fit profession for a gentleman. While widely enjoyed and cultivated on an amateur level, the practice of music was regarded as a pastime. When

Tchaikovsky was born, there was no such thing in Russia as a music school: to become a professional musician was almost by definition to join the ranks of the socially inferior. Worse, it was widely interpreted as a badge of straitened circumstances. The notion of the musician as servant did not die with the bewigged and uniformed Mozart and Haydn; it flourished in parts of Europe well into the twentieth century. By that time, however, it had been laid to rest in Russia itself, as had the notion of 'servant'. But in every country, east or west, it took a very long time for the musical profession even to begin to become fashionable in society at large.

Among the important Russian composers of the nineteenth century—Glinka, Bortnyansky, Dargomyzhsky, Balakirev, Borodin, Mussorgsky, Rimsky-Korsakov—Tchaikovsky was the only one to be conservatoire-trained. On these grounds alone he was initially regarded with the greatest suspicion by the overt nationalists of the 'Mighty Handful' (particularly by the least of them, César Cui), and was never entirely accepted by them. The charge that as a composer he was 'not Russian enough' naturally rankled with Tchaikovsky, but then there was no shortage of those who refused to acknowledge the Rubinstein brothers as 'Russians' at all, owing not to their European training but to their Jewishness.

At the time Tchaikovsky composed his overture *The Storm*, in 1864, he knew neither the music of Schumann nor the number of symphonies Beethoven wrote.

Such was the relative lack of sophistication in Tchaikovsky's early professional environment that at the time he composed his overture **The Storm**, in 1864, he knew neither the music of Schumann nor the number of symphonies Beethoven wrote. Prophetic of later developments, this overture not only uses Russian folksong but shows a gift for colourful, dramatic and brilliantly dazzling orchestration which was already a feature of the Russian 'school', following Glinka's example, and which was to

become one of Tchaikovsky's own greatest assets. Worth noting at this point is that in his use of authentic folksongs, Tchaikovsky actually out-Russianed the 'Mighty Handful'. By the time of his First Symphony, written two years after *The Storm*, he was not only using folksongs but devising wholly original themes derived from the styles, patterns and distinctive feel of Russian folk music in general. A good example is the main theme of the second movement, which bears a distinct relationship to the well-known 'Volga Boat Song' while never actually quoting it. This can be seen as a kind of prototype of the typical Tchaikovskyan 'big tune' – not specifically folk music, but profoundly Russian – that crops up again and again in many works with no overtly Russian reference. The first famous example would be the love theme in *Romeo and Juliet* (1870).

By the time of his First Symphony, written two years after *The Storm*, he was devising wholly original themes derived from the distinctive feel of Russian folk music.

Tchaikovsky was also the first major composer of his generation to write a folk opera (the early, unsuccessful *Voyevoda* of 1868, his most lavishly folk-influenced work); and the three subsequent operas, as we have seen, were also on specifically Russian themes and derived from Russian sources (see Interlude II). In 1876 his views on Russian folk music and its treatment by composers were interestingly set out in a letter to Tolstoy, who had recently sent him a collection of folksongs for possible arrangement (seven years previously Tchaikovsky had arranged fifty for piano duet) or to use as a basis for thematic development.

> *Honoured Count,*
> *Please accept my sincerest thanks for the songs. I must tell you, however, that they have been taken down by an unskilful hand, and in consequence nearly all their original beauty is lost. The chief mistake is that they have been forced artificially into a regular rhythm. Only the Russian dance*

> *songs have a regularly accentuated measure; but the legends [*byliny*] have nothing in common with these. Besides, most of these songs have been forced into the festive key of D major. This is quite out of keeping with the tonality of the genuine Russian folksongs, which are always in some undefined tonality, such as can only be compared with the old church modes. Therefore the songs you have sent are unsuitable for systematic treatment. I could not use them for an album of folksongs, because for this purpose the tunes must be taken down exactly as the people sing them. This is a difficult task, demanding the most delicate musical perception, as well as a great knowledge of musical history. With the exception of Balakirev, and to some extent [*Vasily*] Prokunin, I know of no one who really understands how to do this. But your songs can be used as symphonic material – and excellent material too – of which I shall certainly avail myself at some time in the future.*

Particularly interesting here are his remarks on rhythm, for it was in this realm, more consistently than in any other, that Tchaikovsky mastered the art of repetition without monotony (a powerful feature of his writing, even in such un-folky but deeply Russian works as the Fourth Symphony). Repetition is a cardinal feature not only of Russian folk music but of folk music in general. However, since Tchaikovsky knew very little of non-Russian folk music, his very repetitiousness may be seen as an aspect of his Russianness. This was something of which he himself was well aware.

A further interesting feature of Tchaikovsky's Russianness, particularly as perceived abroad, is the almost total absence (in all his best works) of any reference to the exotic, 'oriental' aspect of Russian culture and geography, so famously exploited in Rimsky-Korsakov's *Scheherazade* and

Mussorgsky's *Pictures at an Exhibition*. That audiences have responded strongly to Tchaikovsky's Russianness without discerning a trace of picture-postcardism is the most potent proof both of its existence and its power.

The **Second Symphony** is even more permeated by Russian characteristics than the First, for actual folksongs are used organically, both as a means of helping to unify large-scale structures and as a basis for development and variation. The last movement, in particular, reflects the seminal role of Glinka in the development of Russian music, and not only in his famous operas *Ruslan and Lyudmila* and *A Life for the Tsar*. Indeed, Tchaikovsky's movement derives from Glinka's single, short orchestral showpiece called *Kamarinskaya*, a kind of mini-precursor of Ravel's *Boléro*, in which a single tune is presented again and again, each time in different instrumental clothing and against a different orchestral background: tone colour, in short, here becomes the primary tool of variation. Of this Tchaikovsky wrote:

> *How astonishingly original is* Kamarinskaya, *from which all the Russian composers who followed [Glinka] (including myself) continue to this day to borrow contrapuntal and harmonic combinations as soon as they have learned to develop a Russian dance tune! This is done unconsciously; but the fact is, Glinka managed to concentrate in this one short work what a dozen second-rate talents would only have invented with the whole expenditure of their powers. Indeed, the entire Russian symphonic tradition could be said to have grown out of* Kamarinskaya, *just as a mighty oak is contained in the tiniest acorn.*

Among the foliage contributed by Tchaikovsky to that Kamarinskayan oak, perhaps the most conspicuous are the

finales of the Second Symphony and the considerably later **Violin Concerto**. Other examples of similar derivation abound, though nowhere does the actual theme come closer to the acorn of *Kamarinskaya* itself than in the Violin Concerto. Chopin, on hearing of a lavish compliment from Liszt, commented, somewhat ruefully: 'Ah, Liszt has made me a country in his Empire.' Tchaikovsky, by contrast, was deeply proud to be a branch of Glinka's oak.

There is more, however, to the Russianness of Russian music than folksong. The Russian Orthodox Church, in the music of its services (and the pealing of bells that precedes and often follows them), made an indelible impression on the national consciousness of most Russians, both urban and rural. The sound and evocation of Russian church bells plays an important part in the music of Mussorgsky, Tchaikovsky, Rachmaninov and others. So does the distinctive and characteristically Russian interval of a falling fourth (as in 'Yo-o, *heave-ho*' in the 'Volga Boat Song'). And so does the combination of deep melancholy and indomitable resilience, reflecting centuries of suffering, oppression, persecution – and hope. All this is to the fore in Tchaikovsky's music. Russian, too, is the near-addiction to narrative. His music fairly bursts at the seams with 'stories': the songs, the operas, the ballets, the 'programme' overtures and fantasies, even the symphonies and the concertos. Tchaikovsky did not have to try consciously to be Russian: he simply couldn't help it. In that famous passage about Glinka, he himself alludes to the power of the unconscious in musical creation. But his lifelong, restless, often aimless wanderings in Europe and America also served to sharpen and intensify his consciousness of Russianness. Ultimately, though, Tchaikovsky the composer was not a

His music fairly bursts at the seams with 'stories': the songs, the operas, the ballets, the 'programme' overtures and fantasies, even the symphonies and the concertos.

Chapter 7

Morbidity, Mortality and Myth 1891–1893

Morbidity, Mortality and Myth 1891–1893

On his return to Russia in June, Tchaikovsky was at last able to complete the one-act opera and the new ballet commissioned before his departure for America. Sadly neither was a success – for the moment. The opera *Iolanta* was poorly received, and has never gained even moderate popularity. The ballet, based on a story by E.T.A. Hoffmann, was also poorly received, but it did provide Tchaikovsky with what may well be his most popular orchestral work: **The Nutcracker** suite. And the ballet itself soon followed suit.

To this day, the celesta has never been more famously used than in the 'Dance of the Sugar-Plum Fairy.'

Rumour has it that this, or at least the original ballet, was the first work by a major composer to include the newly invented celesta (or céleste). This isn't quite true. Tchaikovsky himself had used it in an earlier, though very recent, work (*Voyevoda* – see below), and the instrument had been invented almost seven years before that. However, even to this day, it has never been more famously used than in the 'Dance of the Sugar-Plum Fairy'.

The reason Tchaikovsky compiled *The Nutcracker* suite at all was to replace a work written around the time of Mme von Meck's bombshell, and which he had later destroyed, after a single performance: his 'symphonic ballad' *Voyevoda*. (This was unrelated, surprisingly, to his earlier opera of the same name.) Fortunately, he was an incompetent, or histrionic, exterminator. While he destroyed the actual orchestral score, he neglected to dispose of the individual instrumental parts prepared for that one performance. It was thus easily reconstructed after his death, adding to the repertoire one of his most interesting and substantial orchestral works – though performances of it today are rare. For all the disjunction that often appears between a work and the circumstances of its creation, it seems hardly conceivable that the darkness of this one is not directly related to the effect of Mme von Meck's letter. The mere association of the two would have been enough to turn Tchaikovsky against it. But there was more to it than that. He was also afraid – not for the first time – that the work revealed him as a composer whose powers were deserting him.

What *Voyevoda* does reveal (unlike *The Nutcracker* suite) is an increasing gloom, a kind of pessimistic fatalism which had certainly surfaced before, in works like the Fourth and Fifth Symphonies, but which was now beginning to take centre stage in Tchaikovsky's music. Certainly the gloom of *Voyevoda* anticipates the even greater gloom of the Sixth Symphony, one of the most pessimistic pieces of music ever written; but it affected neither the enormous esteem in which Tchaikovsky was now held throughout the musical world nor the tremendous affection that audiences and players alike had for him. As a conductor, he had come a long way from the incompetent fledgling at the Conservatoire – he who had had to hold his head on. There were other ways of losing it, however, which stayed with him. A choir member in St Petersburg remembered a particularly notable rehearsal near the end of Tchaikovsky's life:

The gloom of *Voyevoda* anticipates the even greater gloom of the Sixth Symphony, one of the most pessimistic pieces of music ever written.

> *Taunted by the more rebellious elements in the choir, Pyotr Il'yich finally lost his presence of mind. He fairly bellowed at us, gesticulating so wildly with his baton that it finally broke, one end shooting off into one of the choirs; but these thunderous outbursts were permeated with such exceptional good nature, such immeasurable Russian mildness that it was impossible to get angry with the conductor, the more so since his situation was in reality very difficult.*

The notion of a violent rage permeated with good will and mildness is perhaps a little elusive, but there's no doubting that on this occasion Tchaikovsky was indeed in a difficult situation – and not only with the choir:

> *The orchestra, being used to playing without a choir, became confused, and we were slow in coming in after the soloists. First the basses weren't there, then the tenors got lost, then the drum made a mess of everything. In the end, though, it all went amazingly smoothly. We sang well at the final rehearsal, and even better at the concert. But we owed it all to Tchaikovsky, who had taken such exceptional pains with us. His gentle simplicity, his good-natured reprimands, and the whole tone in which he delivered both his reproofs and his encouragements won him the hearts of all who worked under him.*

But there were times when he felt out of his depth, even in his own music. One unique instance was a performance of *Eugene Onegin*, which he was to have conducted in Hamburg. 'They had learnt the work very thoroughly,' he recalled, 'and the production was not at all bad, but there were changes in the recitatives due to the German text and I couldn't help getting lost and muddling it. Despite all their attempts to persuade me, I withdrew from conducting it because I was frankly terrified of ruining the whole thing. Especially since the regular conductor there isn't just some middling provincial: he's a positive genius, and he was dying to conduct the first performance. They call him Mahler.'

'I withdrew from conducting because I was frankly terrified of ruining the whole thing. Especially since the regular conductor there isn't some middling provincial; he's a positive genius. They call him Mahler.'

Tchaikovsky was now at the apex of his international celebrity. In France he was elected a 'corresponding member' of the Académie Française. But this honour paled in his memory next to a visit he made on the way to receiving it in late December 1892. He paid a call on Fanny Dürbach, whom as a child he had loved second only to his mother, and who had been the most important influence on his creative development between the ages of four and eight. After more than forty years, it was with more than a little trepidation that he stood on the step and rang the bell. He needn't have worried:

Mlle Fanny herself came to the door, and I recognised her at once. Despite her seventy years, which one can scarcely believe, she had altered amazingly little. That same high-coloured complexion and the soft brown eyes – and her hair is hardly grey at all, though she has grown much stouter. I had dreaded tears and an emotional scene, but there was nothing of the kind. She greeted me as though it had been one year rather than forty – joyfully and tenderly, but with affecting simplicity. It was clear to me at once why we had all loved her so. Naturally we started with reminiscences, and she recalled many interesting details from my childhood. Then she showed me our copybooks, my exercises, and letters, and – what was of the greatest interest to me – a few dear, kind letters from our mother. I can hardly describe what a strange and wonderful feeling came over me while listening to her recollections and looking over these letters and books. The past rose up so vividly before me that I seemed to inhale the air of Votkinsk and hear our mother's voice as though she were there in the room with us. I stayed from three until eight o'clock, without noticing the time, and spent the whole of the next day in her company. In the evening I embraced her when I left, and promised to come back one day.

On his return to Russia, the newly decorated composer was welcomed as a national hero, which in fact he had been for some time. In Odessa alone, in addition to his professional commitments, he was subjected to almost a fortnight of parties, dinners and celebrations. Inevitably it left him feeling exhausted:

'They are honouring me here as if I were some great man, almost the saviour of the fatherland, and I am so pulled about in all directions that I can scarcely breathe.'

I have never experienced the like of what is happening just now. They are honouring me here as if I were some great man, almost the saviour of the fatherland, and I am so pulled about in all directions that I can scarcely breathe. I've been here nearly two weeks now and in that time I have managed to conduct at five concerts, take innumerable rehearsals, and consume dozens of dinners and suppers given in my honour. It's all very tiring but it would be ridiculous to complain because eventually I shall be so glad to look back on all the enthusiasm and incredible ovations. I have also supervised the rehearsals of The Queen of Spades *and I attended the three performances. I thank God for the health that I command and which enables me to survive this sort of life for a full two weeks. I have never received such praise anywhere. If only I might at some stage be given in Moscow or Petersburg even a fraction of what I was accorded in Odessa!*

It was on the way home from Odessa that he decided to go ahead with an idea for his next symphony, which he had mapped out some months earlier. Hardly had he begun composing it, however, than he accepted the offer of an honorary doctorate from Cambridge University. In the interim between his return home and his departure for England, he was, by all accounts, in particularly cheerful and outgoing spirits. Never had he appeared happier.

After a week in St Petersburg, Tchaikovsky set off for England, where he would meet Saint-Saëns and Grieg again,

Tchaikovsky with his nephew Vladimir Levovich 'Bob' Davïdov, 1892

as well as Arrigo Boito and Max Bruch, all of whom were being similarly honoured. Characteristically, almost as soon as he left Russia he was overcome with homesickness. This time it was acutely focused on Bob, who was preparing for his final exams at the School of Jurisprudence. From Berlin, on 15 May 1893, Tchaikovsky unburdened himself with his usual abandon: 'This time, probably due to memories of our journey together last year, I have been overcome with yearnings, and suffered and wept more than ever. It's really kind of psychopathic.' It got worse. His appetite went completely, he was racked by insomnia, and but for the shame and embarrassment it would have entailed he might well have turned back. Two days later he arrived in London, with Bob still very much on his mind:

> *I write to you with a sort of voluptuousness. The thought that this letter will be in your hands, at home, makes me deeply happy yet it also makes me weep. Why, oh why do I subject myself to these ordeals? I suffer not only from an anguish quite inexpressible in words (though in my new symphony there's a passage that expresses it quite well) but also from a horror of strangers, from some vague dread and the devil knows what else. And this condition manifests itself physically, in a pain in the pit of my stomach and an aching and a weakness in my legs.*

In the event, he quite enjoyed himself; he liked Cambridge and made new friends, and the ceremony was clearly to his taste:

> *We were attired in ample robes, scarlet and white, with full sleeves, and on our heads, college caps of black velvet with gold tassels. Thus decked out, we processed through the town, under*

Tchaikovsky receiving an honorary doctorate from Cambridge University, 1893

> *a tropical sun. At the head of the group of went the Maharajah of Bohonager in a turban of cloth sparkling with fabulous jewels and a diamond necklace. Dare I confess that, as the enemy of the commonplace, and of the neuter tints of our modern garb, I was enchanted with this adventure? The people stood on each side of the railings, and cheered us with great enthusiasm. Meanwhile the Senate House, in which the degrees were conferred, had become crowded with undergraduates and guests. The former were not merely spectators, but – as we afterwards discovered – participants in the event. When the Vice-Chancellor and other members of the Senate had taken their places, the ceremony began. Each recipient rises in turn from his seat, while the public orator recounts his claims to recognition in a Latin oration. Here the undergraduates begin to play their part. According to ancient tradition, they are allowed to hiss, cheer, and make jokes at the expense of the new doctors. At every joke the orator waits until the noise and laughter has subsided, and then continues to read aloud. When this is done, the recipient is led up to the Vice-Chancellor, who greets him as doctor* in nomine Patri, Filii et Spiritus Sancti.

Tchaikovsky noted that this Christian formula was judiciously omitted in the case of the Maharajah of Bohonager.

His return to Russia was clouded by bad news. Two close friends had died; two more were on the point of death (one of them being Nikolay Zverev, the teacher of Rachmaninov). Whereas in former times this catalogue of loss would have all but unhinged him, now, though obviously saddened and distressed, he took it in his stride. His main preoccupation was with his new symphony. It was to be what he described simply as a 'programme symphony'. But, provocatively, this was a 'programme' that the composer would announce but never explain. It went with him, as intended, to the grave.

He did, however, confess to Modest that it was 'so intensely personal that during my travels, while composing it in my mind, I shed many, many tears.'

Given Tchaikovsky's death so soon after the premiere, the extra-musical meaning of the work has been variously interpreted and hotly contested, though in view of the composer's own testimony a strongly, indeed fundamentally, autobiographical component would seem to be incontestable. The outstanding questions must be: How much? How specific? How self-consciously prophetic? Whether by design or through oversight, Tchaikovsky left a few posthumous clues. In one of his preparatory notebooks, found after his death, he wrote:

> *The ultimate essence of the plan is LIFE. First movement – all impulse, confidence, thirst for activity. Must be short. (Finale, death – result of collapse.) Second movement, LOVE; third, disappointment; fourth ends with a dying away (also short).*

On another, separate sheet, containing musical sketches, we find a different but related summary: 'Life. (1) Youth. (II) Obstacles!' Above the following bar he wrote 'Nonsense!' and later, 'Coda. Forward, forward!' In the context of some earlier sketches, he scribbled, 'A motif: for what? For what? Why? Beginning and main idea of whole symphony.' It would seem that, whatever its final form, it took some time to congeal, even in the mind of the composer.

Well before conceiving the work, Tchaikovsky had written to Mme von Meck, in 1878, about the whole nature of programme music, and his remarks bear re-airing. The inspiration of a symphonic composer, he explained, could be either subjective or objective:

> *In the first instance, he uses his music to express his own feelings, joys, sufferings; in short, like a lyric poet he pours out his own soul, so to speak. In this instance, a programme is not only unnecessary, but even impossible. But it is another matter when a musician, reading a poetic work or struck by a scene in nature, wishes to express in musical form that subject that has kindled his inspiration. Here a programme is essential . . . In any event, to my mind both sorts possess completely identical* raisons d'être *. . . It goes without saying that not every subject is fit for a symphony, just as not every subject is fit for an opera – but still programme music can and must exist, just as it is impossible to demand that literature make do without the epic element and limit itself to lyricism alone.*

As happened when composing *The Sorceress* and *The Sleeping Beauty*, the work, to begin with, fairly tumbled out of him: 'When I got back, I settled to the sketches and worked with such fervour and speed that in less than four days I had completed the first movement and already had a clear idea of the others.' In common with many highly creative artists, there were moments when it was not always clear whether he was composing the music or the music was composing him, as it were. The passivity of creation is one of life's most fascinating mysteries. Think only of Stravinsky on composing *The Rite of Spring*: 'I was guided by no system whatsoever when I composed *The Rite*. I heard, and I wrote what I heard. I am the vessel through which *The Rite* passed.' An astonishing confession. Tchaikovsky's experience was nothing like so dramatic, but the work was still taking him by surprise. As he told Modest, 'Everything is coming out different from how I had imagined it.' In this case, however, he seemed almost serenely unconcerned about its eventual reception:

In common with many highly creative artists, there were moments when it was not always clear whether Tchaikovsky was composing the music or the music was composing him.

> *It will be perfectly normal and unsurprising if the piece is not truly understood, or is even traduced by the critics. It would hardly be the first time. But I myself am in no doubt whatever that this is far and away the best, and in particular, the most sincere of all my pieces. I love it as I have never loved any of my other musical progeny.*

But again, the speed of creation slowed drastically when it came to the orchestration.

> *The further I go, the more difficult it becomes. Twenty years ago I should have rushed it through without a second thought, and it would have turned out fine. Now I am turning coward, not because my powers are declining in old age but because I have become far more severe on myself and have quite lost my former self-confidence. I have been sitting all day over two pages, yet they simply will not come out as I wish. In spite of this, however, the work continues to progress. Indeed I have never been so pleased with myself before – so proud, so joyful in the knowledge that I have here done something really good.*

The fact that he refers to himself in terms of 'old age' is both ironic and prophetic. He was, after all, only fifty-three. But it was as close as he got. Nine days after conducting the premiere, he was dead.

Well over a century later, the cause of his death remains a matter of the most heated controversy. According to tradition, he died of cholera, after drinking a glass of unboiled water in a restaurant. (The restaurant evidence doesn't stack up, but the unboiled water is entirely plausible. Modest observes that of all serious diseases Tchaikovsky

The cause of his death remains a matter of heated controversy. According to gossip, subsequently buttressed by scholarly evidence, he committed suicide.

was least afraid of cholera, despite the fact that it was this that carried off his mother.) According to gossip, subsequently buttressed by scholarly evidence, he committed suicide. Various possible motives have been cited, all of them connected in one way or another with his homosexuality. Both versions, as it happens, raise numerous questions, and the literature is more confusing than helpful. In one of the most widely read and authoritative books on the composer, the author writes: 'That Tchaikovsky committed suicide is beyond dispute.'

On the contrary: it has been very persuasively disputed, with a battery of scholarly documentation. Why should Tchaikovsky have committed suicide when he was at the very peak of both his powers and his popularity? We have it on the authority of his brother Modest (and this is corroborated by others) that 'in spite of the distressing news which met him in all directions on his homecoming, from the time of his return from England to the end of his life, Tchaikovsky was as serene and cheerful as at any period in his existence.' Despite the gloom of the Sixth Symphony, he was widely observed to be in generally high spirits, all the more so after completing with joy and pride what he regarded as his finest work. Nor is there any persuasive evidence that he was ever really suicidally minded. Idle talk of ending one's life, such as occurs several times in his correspondence, was part of the common change of Romantic parlance throughout Europe, beginning with Goethe's *The Sorrows of Young Werther* in the eighteenth century and flourishing, in certain circles, until the outbreak of the First World War. The one (improbable) suicide story we have – Tchaikovsky's supposed attempt to contract pneumonia by wading into the Moscow River – is based, as noted earlier, on a single, unreliable source, written decades after the incident was alleged to have taken place. Nor should

Despite the gloom of the Sixth Symphony, he was generally high spirits. Nor is there any persuasive evidence that he was ever really suicidally minded.

we forget that he weathered that storm, by far the severest crisis in his life, and emerged stronger as both artist and man (albeit with all his neuroses intact). One looks in vain for anything remotely comparable in the last years of his life, unless one admits speculative foreboding over the future of his relationship with Bob, for which there is certainly some evidence.

In connection with Tchaikovsky's attitudes to life and death, it is interesting to read a letter written nine years earlier, to his cousin Anna Merkling, after her congratulations on his forty-fourth birthday:

> *Many thanks, dear Anna, for thinking of me. Without bitterness, I receive congratulations upon the fact that I am now a year older! I have no wish to die, and I desire to attain a ripe old age; nor would I willingly have my youth back and go through life again. Once is enough! The past, of which you speak with regret, I too regret, for no one likes better to be lost in memories of old days, no one feels more keenly the emptiness and brevity of life – but I do not wish to be young again. I cannot but feel that the sum total of good which I enjoy at present is far, far greater than that which stood to my credit in youth: therefore I do not in the least regret my four-and-forty years. Nor sixty, nor seventy, provided I am still physically sound and in possession of my mental faculties! At the same time one ought not to fear death. In this respect, however, I am in no position to boast. I am not sufficiently infused by religion to regard death as the beginning of a new life, nor am I sufficiently philosophical to be satisfied with the prospect of annihilation. In this respect I envy no one so much as the religious man.*

According to what remains the most widely accepted account of his death, however, he committed suicide, not by his own choice but because he was 'sentenced' so to do by a secretly convened 'court of honour' with no legal jurisdiction whatever. The scenario proceeds as follows: a letter was written to the tsar by a certain Duke Stenbok-Fermor, reporting Tchaikovsky's supposed seduction of his young nephew. The man entrusted with the delivery of this letter, fully aware of its contents, had been a contemporary of Tchaikovsky's at the School of Jurisprudence. Appalled at the dishonour this would bring on the School and its 'old boys,' this gentleman – one Nikolay Jacobi – decided not to deliver the letter to the tsar at all. Instead, he convened the aforementioned 'court,' comprising seven of Tchaikovsky's former school friends. The composer was summoned to a 'hearing,' and in order to preserve the school from scandal was 'required' (their term) to take his own life.

The pettiness and fatuity of such a course aside, its supposed consequence strains credulity, whatever the weight of scholarship behind it (and that itself is hotly debated). Would the most famous Russian composer in history, then at the peak of his career, with friends in high places (not excepting the tsar himself) and in many countries, meekly have accepted this verdict and simply done as he was told? True, he passionately loved Russia and often felt acutely homesick when abroad. Exile, even in luxury, might well have proved intolerable, but would he have dismissed it without a try? Had the price of exile proved more than he could bear, he might commit suicide then, but not before. Besides, was his art not a higher priority? It had proved so before. Nor is there any certainty that the tsar would actually have unleashed a scandal. Homosexuality in Russia, as elsewhere, was commonplace, though not openly acknowledged, and the courts appear generally to have turned a blind eye to it, as might the tsar have –

Homosexuality in Russia, as elsewhere, was commonplace, though not openly acknowledged. Many of the tsar's own relatives and highest officials were also homosexual.

especially in the case of Tchaikovsky, one of the brightest jewels in Russia's national crown. In fact many of the tsar's own relatives and highest officials were also homosexual – as Tchaikovsky and his 'judges' were perfectly well aware.

But even supposing the suicide theory to be true, would the physically squeamish Tchaikovsky – remember the incident of the boa-constrictor – really have chosen to infect himself with cholera, knowing that he would be guaranteed days of appalling suffering (exacerbated by prolonged and severe diarrhoea and vomiting), and that he would cause protracted, even agonising, distress to his family and closest friends? The same question can be asked in the context of the alternative theory of arsenic poisoning. There is no evidence that Tchaikovsky was a masochist, and his lifelong solicitude for the wellbeing of those close to him is a matter of record. In any case, the doctors attending him in his last days, the brothers Lev and Vasily Bertenson (two of the foremost physicians in St Petersburg), were agreed in their diagnosis of cholera. Whatever the cause, he endured four days of intermittent agony before his life was done. It seems only fitting that the account of them should be left to his brother Modest, who was there:

> *His courage was wonderful, and in the intervals between the paroxysms of pain he made little jokes with those around him. He constantly begged his nurses to take some rest, and was grateful for the smallest service. On Friday his condition seemed more hopeful, and he himself believed he had been 'snatched from the jaws of death.' But on the following day his mental depression returned. 'Leave me,' he said to his doctors, 'you can do no good. I shall never recover.' Gradually he passed into the second stage of cholera, with its most dangerous symptom – complete inactivity of the kidneys. He slept more, but his sleep was restless, and sometimes*

he wandered in his mind. At these times he continually repeated the name of Nadezhda Filaretovna von Meck in an indignant, or reproachful, tone. Consciousness returned at longer intervals, and when his servant Alexis arrived, he was no longer able to recognise him. A warm bath was tried as a last resource, but without avail, and soon afterwards his pulse grew so weak that the end seemed imminent. At the desire of his brother Nikolay, a priest was sent for from St Isaac's Cathedral. He did not administer the sacrament, as Tchaikovsky was now quite unconscious, but prayed in clear and distinct tones, which, however, did not seem to reach the ears of the dying man. At three o'clock on the morning of 25 October [6 November], Tchaikovsky died in the presence of three doctors, the two Litke brothers, Buxhövden, our nephew [Bob] Davïdov, my brother's faithful valet Alexis Sofronov, my own valet Nazar Litrov,

Tchaikovsky on his deathbed, 1893

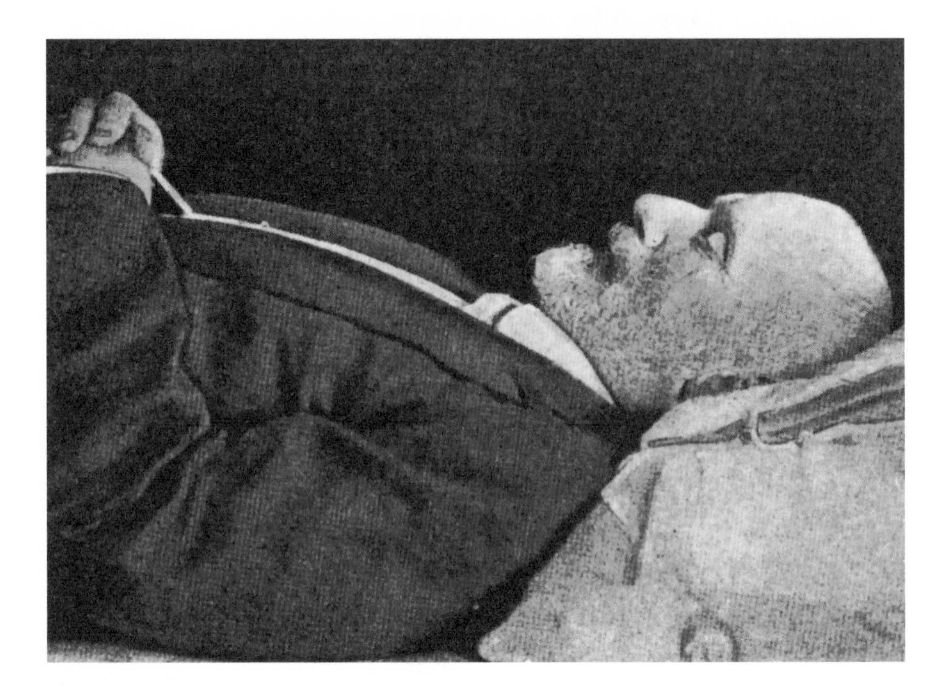

> *the medical attendant, our brother Nikolay and I. At the last moment an indescribable look of recognition lit up his face – a gleam that died only with his last breath.*

Tchaikovsky was dead, and the music lovers of three continents struggled to believe it. The tsar himself insisted on meeting the burial costs and instructed the Directorate of the Imperial Theatres to organise the funeral. A magnificent service was held in the Kazan Cathedral in St Petersburg. 6,000 mourners filled the church, while 60,000 thronged the streets outside. The tsar himself did not attend (that would have been unprecedented), but he sent an elaborate wreath of white roses; it complemented the white cassocks of the clergy as they marched in front of the hearse, which was drawn by six horses.

At five o'clock in the afternoon of Thursday 28 October 1893, Tchaikovsky's coffin was lowered into the grave at the cemetery of the Alexander Nevsky Monastery, not far from those of Borodin and Mussorgsky. His life was over. The life of his music, on the other hand, was just beginning. He may have been too modest to entertain the thought, but nothing would have given him more joy than to realise that well after a century later his works would still be played and loved by many thousands, many millions, of music lovers around the world. He was a man who could well have written of his entire life's work what Beethoven wrote on the first page of his *Missa solemnis*: 'From the heart; may it go to the heart'. Like all great composers, he has proved immortal.

Nothing would have given Tchaikovsky more joy than to realise that well after a century later his works would still be played and loved by many thousands, many millions, of music lovers around the world.

Epilogue: Tchaikovsky and Posterity

Posterity is a fickle mistress – more to the point, a fickle lover – and very often, in the long run (the only perspective in which posterity counts) it is the public, not the critics or 'connoisseurs', who have set the agenda. Eventually, the pundits concur that the public got it right. Music, however, is intrinsically and inevitably a subjective experience, and 'right' remains a purely personal judgement. There is nothing approaching a universally accepted 'objective' standard by which music can be 'proved' to be good or otherwise. There are many reasons for this, and they could sustain a lengthy book, but one of them is that music fulfils such an immense variety of functions. It may be perfect for one of them but next to useless for all the others. But what any thorough acquaintance with critical history affirms unequivocally is that the only music to last through centuries is music that speaks both to and of people: music that addresses and reflects human experience. Tchaikovsky understood this, and was specifically, though not exclusively, motivated by it.

The fate of his music, where critical commentary is concerned, has been wildly, sometimes hysterically, inconsistent.

From the beginning Tchaikovsky struck a chord with audiences, and that has hardly varied. The fate of his music, where critical commentary is concerned, has been wildly, sometimes hysterically, inconsistent – and in one sense unique: no great composer's character has been more lavishly traduced (not to say libelled) on the ostensible basis of his music alone. When Eduard Hanslick wrote, in 1881, that the Violin Concerto 'stinks to the ear', he was indulging in the standard critical confusion of opinion and analysis, but at least he kept (if only loosely) to his appointed task: for better or worse, he was writing about the music. But what do we make of the widely (and on the whole deservedly) respected mid-twentieth-century English critic who wrote: 'This man is ill, we feel. Must we be shown all his sores, without exception?' And it is not clear what illumination of a musical kind we can derive from the 'observation' of another twentieth-century English critic that Tchaikovsky's music 'reflects all the indulgent yearning and garish exteriorisation of a composer who can never refrain from wearing his heart on his sleeve – if, indeed, it is not music which suggests a less modest image than that.' Since when can music, the least specifically descriptive of all the arts, suggest such 'less modest' images? And let us not sully our minds by considering what these 'less modest' images might be. Elsewhere we read of Tchaikovsky 'gushing like a schoolgirl', that 'the man and his music are one: unsatisfied and inflamed'; we read of the 'effeminacy' and 'weakness' of Tchaikovsky, and we learn from the American critic James Huneker, writing as early as 1905 (barely a decade after Tchaikovsky's death), that some of the composer's music is 'truly pathological.'

When Eduard Hanslick wrote that the Violin Concerto 'stinks to the ear', at least he kept to his appointed task: for better or worse, he was writing about the music.

The subtext of all these remarks, barring only Hanslick's, is Tchaikovsky's much-vaunted homosexuality. It would be easy to blame all this on the legacy of Sigmund Freud, whose influence in the West, now much diminished, was once pervasive. Yet our palpable obsession with life below the belt (no longer a matter of the subconscious) does not extend, where music is concerned, to heterosexual composers. Where do we read of phallic symbolism and unbecoming masculinity and strength in the music of Liszt or Wagner? (There is an unmistakable representation of sexual intercourse in *Tristan und Isolde*, but this has not led to an ejaculation of critical opprobrium over 'immodest' images, let alone pathology – indeed it has eluded widespread comment.) Nor has the sexual perversion of criticism been confined to countries where Freud's teachings once held sway. In the Soviet Union, where Tchaikovsky's music and reputation were routinely vilified by Communist critics until the centenary of his birth in 1940, obsession with his sexuality resulted in the wholesale suppression of all information pertaining to it, particularly after his post-centenary 'rehabilitation' as a Soviet icon. Thus was Tchaikovsky scholarship stunted from birth. Fortunately, the copious evidence was not destroyed but merely locked away under layers of bureaucratic obstruction. This, however, was powerless to prevent a flourishing subculture of gossip.

Tchaikovsky's posthumous troubles in his own land were by no means confined to problems with sexuality. As an avowed monarchist and natural conservative who openly deplored socialist doctrines – and, also, of course, as a western-influenced composer much fêted abroad – he was condemned after the Russian Revolution as a decadent bourgeois reactionary whose music was irrelevant if not downright harmful to the workers. The last people to heed this message, however, were musicians and those selfsame workers who thronged to concerts of Tchaikovsky's music, stamping, clapping and roaring their approval. Like Shostakovich after him, Tchaikovsky demonstrated through music alone the futility of attempting to chain the human spirit. Before the Revolution, his music was promoted far and wide. In 1910, the conductor Serge Koussevitzky took

Like Shostakovich after him, Tchaikovsky demonstrated through music alone the futility of attempting to chain the human spirit.

his orchestra up and down the River Volga on a chartered steamboat, bringing symphonic music – Tchaikovsky's figured prominently – to places where it had scarcely even been heard of, let alone heard. He repeated these tours in 1912 and 1914, leaving an indelible image.

Meanwhile, Tchaikovsky's influence on composers proceeded apace, and not only on Russians. Such outwardly polar opposites as Rachmaninov and Stravinsky were profoundly influenced by Tchaikovsky, though in very different ways; so, to a lesser extent, was Shostakovich (though Prokofiev was not). Less obvious, perhaps, but no less demonstrable, is his influence on such disparate composers as Mahler, Puccini, Sibelius, Berg and Schnittke. Nor has his influence been confined to the concert hall, the ballet stage and the opera house. Where it has been felt most widely of all is in the realm of film music. Before the advent of the 'talkies' in 1927, Tchaikovsky was often the sole source of the accompanying music in cinemas – both in the posh ones with their house orchestras, and in the 'flea pits' with their lone pianists. In the heydays of Hollywood, indeed in the scores of John Williams, James Horner, Howard Shore and others in our own time, the ghost of Tchaikovsky is seldom very far away (though the godfather of sinister, 'twisted', horror-orientated film music has traditionally been the perennially 'unpopular' Arnold Schoenberg). The cinematic offspring of the 'Love Theme' from Tchaikovsky's *Romeo and Juliet* and similar passages have long since become uncountable, and the *1812* festival overture of 1880 was a Hollywood blockbuster hungering for the invention of film. Indeed, the history of film music without Tchaikovsky would be almost unthinkable – which is to the discredit of neither.

The history of film music without Tchaikovsky would be almost unthinkable – which is to the discredit of neither.

Because he dealt with, and embodied, extremes of emotion, Tchaikovsky's music is destined always to be controversial, as is

Wagner's. But in the climate of the early twenty-first century it stands a better chance than ever of being accepted, or rejected, on the basis of what it is, rather than what it represents. It is not homosexual music, or socialist or bourgeois or ultimately even Russian music. These things are all extraneous and finally irrelevant. It is music: not always plain or simple, but always very human. Its humanity, like its composer, embraced both the noble and profound, and the trite and superficial, all expressed with a fundamental honesty that transcended matters of mere sincerity. As an artist, Tchaikovsky was first, last and always a musician, for whom musicianship, and music itself, was paramount. He did not always succeed. When he failed, it was seldom for want of aspiration. But he will live on through his best music, which reveals a great musician, a consummate craftsman, a powerful, often original, mind, and a great and generous heart. Unless some malign ideology succeeds in dehumanising the human spirit altogether, we will always have need of such people.

As an artist, Tchaikovsky was first, last and always a musician, for whom musicianship, and music itself, was paramount.

The Western Background

Overview

The nineteenth century, especially in Europe and North America, was an era of unprecedented change, peppered, inevitably, with wars and revolutions of almost every kind and at every level of society. The continuing advance of the Industrial Revolution, while far from abolishing poverty, brought new wealth to an ever-expanding middle class. Factories proliferated throughout Europe, soon exceeding the supply of local raw materials and thereby intensifying the impulse towards colonisation. Europe's great political and industrial powers, especially Britain and France (and later in the century Germany), together with other countries such as Portugal and Spain (and then Belgium and Italy), were carving up the African continent, conscious of its wealth of natural resources. Despite growing public unease, the slave trade continued, though its days were numbered. The British outlawed slave trading in 1807, but slavery itself was not made illegal until Parliament passed the Abolition of Slavery Act in 1833. Other European countries followed suit, though it was not until 1870 that the last slave was shipped to the Americas.

Alarmed by European expansionism, China and Japan attempted to shut out the West altogether, but this did nothing to stop European empire building, which went on apace as one consequence of the Napoleonic Wars (1799–1815). The wars also had the effect of igniting a nationalist fervour in countries from Italy to Russia. This nationalism became a running feature of the century as a whole. In 1848, revolutions broke out all over Europe, and Karl Marx and Friedrich Engels published their epoch-making Communist Manifesto. Revolutions in Latin America resulted in a spate of new countries whose territorial disputes led to wars with each other. Of more lasting significance, in world terms, was the Crimean War (1853–6), in which Russia, Turkey, France, Austria and Sardinia (which included Piedmont) scrambled for territory as the Ottoman Empire began to collapse. Equally significant was the American Civil War (1861–5), which brought slavery to an end in the United States. A major consequence of the Austro-Prussian War (1866), which followed Bismarck's dissolution of the German Confederation, was the creation of a single German state and the formation of Austria-Hungary as a dual monarchy. Further series of conflicts led to the establishment of modern Italy in 1871, and the Franco-Prussian War (1870–71) flared up over the question of European leadership. In the Balkans, the Russo-Turkish War (1877–8) was fought over the matter of who was to control the peninsula.

Nationalist fervour became a running feature of the nineteenth century as a whole.

In 1837, Queen Victoria began a reign lasting more than sixty-three years. As she ruled over the most far-flung empire ever known (encompassing more than a quarter of the world's lands and people), her monarchical powers at home were steadily reduced until they ended up being largely symbolic. This shift of authority was accompanied by an increasing number of educated people, among whom were many men with the newly acquired right to vote.

By the time of Victoria's death in January 1901, the world had changed more dramatically than in any previous century.

Absolute monarchies had become the rare exception rather than the rule, workers in many countries had achieved conditions and rights beyond the dreams of their grandparents, literacy rates had quadrupled, trade unions were established and recognised (in Germany, Britain and France), the Civil Rights Act had made citizens of all American blacks, effective socialist parties had been formed in many countries, child labour had been largely eradicated, women's rights had come to the fore, and more than twenty-eight million people had cut their links with Europe and emigrated to America. These people contributed to the emergence of the United States as one of the world's greatest industrial and political powers.

Science and Technology

As in the previous century, science and technology continued to expand human knowledge during the nineteenth century, but to an unprecedented degree. In 1801, when Joseph Lalande published his *Histoire céleste française* (which catalogues 47,390 stars), he heralded a century of astronomical discovery both literal and figurative, not least on the medical front. The single greatest advance in medicine – led by Louis Pasteur in France and Robert Koch in Germany – was undoubtedly the discovery that bacteria and viruses lead to infection. Their work resulted in mass immunisation and inoculation programmes against more than twenty diseases, including such rapacious killers as smallpox, tuberculosis and cholera (the last having claimed more than 16,000 people in London alone in 1849). Other landmarks included the discovery of quinine as a cure for malaria, the introduction of ether as an anaesthetic in 1847 (which with increased use of antiseptics resulted in

> Science and technology continued to expand human knowledge during the nineteenth century, to an unprecedented degree.

unprecedented advances in surgery), and the development of X-ray therapy in 1895. This last scientific advance revolutionised the diagnosis of illnesses and injuries, thereby saving and prolonging millions of future lives.

Nineteenth-century developments also included: mass production of steel; the birth and development of railways, both above and below ground, with incalculable effects on almost every branch of civilisation (and warfare); the discovery and widespread dissemination of electricity as a major power source; the advent of the telephone, the bicycle, the washing machine, the typewriter, the gramophone; the transmission of radio waves; and the oil drill. Indeed, towards the end of the century, electricity and oil were challenging the supremacy of coal and steam as the principal fuels for machines, leading to the invention of the internal combustion engine and hence also the motor car and the manufacture of plastics and artificial rubber.

Arms and Munitions

As ever, arms and munitions played a key part in most of the world's developed economies. By the middle of the century, the Krupp factory in Essen had become the world's leading arms manufacturer, producing its first cast steel cannon in 1847. In 1853 Samuel Colt, inventor of the single-barrelled pistol, revolutionised the small arms business in the United States, working also on submarine mines and telegraphy; Richard Gatling, a trained physician, contributed to death and destruction in the American Civil War with his monstrous ten-barrelled gun, firing 1,200 shots a minute (a precursor of the Maxim machine gun of 1882). But ploughshares flourished too.

Agriculture

Although agriculture was easily sidelined by the achievements of the Industrial Revolution, it experienced revolutions of its own, with breeding experiments leading to bigger crop yields and fatter animals. Cyrus McCormick invented his reaping machine in America in 1831, heralding a new age of mechanised harvesting. Justus von Liebig's *Organic Chemistry in its Application to Agriculture and Physiology* (1840) inaugurated the age of scientific farming and the subsequent use of artificial fertilisers in 1855. Agricultural colleges began to proliferate from the 1850s onwards, and by the last quarter of the century refrigerated ships were plying the Atlantic, leading to worldwide food markets (long before the establishment of domestic refrigerators).

Trade

In the 1840s Britain's adoption of a free trade policy (no customs duties) helped to establish London as the centre of world trade, with the pound sterling as the dominant currency. By the 1870s many other countries had introduced import levies as a means of protecting their own industries from economic imperialism. Regular steamship services were established between California and the Far East, and gunrunning became a worldwide industry. On the domestic front, the invention of tinned foods and the advent of department stores in the second half of the century transformed the daily lives of countless housewives and domestics.

Britain's adoption of a free trade policy helped to establish London as the centre of world trade.

Ideas

As might be expected in a time of such ferment, the century was rich in philosophers, though the ideas that had (and continue to have) the most impact came from other quarters. The high ground was held by the Germans, much as the French had held it in the previous century. The great names are G.W.F. Hegel (1770–1831), Arthur Schopenhauer (1788–1860) and Friedrich Nietzsche (1844–1900), all of whom were much concerned with music in one way or another. Nor should one forget the Danish Søren Kierkegaard (1813–1855).

Hegel argued that consciousness and the world of external objects were inseparable aspects of a single whole, and that truth is discoverable only through a dialectic process of contradiction and resolution – a thoroughly rationalist idea with clear parallels in the concept of sonata form.

Schopenhauer took a more pessimistic view (and one more in keeping with the preoccupations of the Romantics), in which the irrational will is seen as the governing principle of our perception, dominated by an endless cycle of desire and frustration from which the only escape is aesthetic contemplation.

His thinking had a powerful effect on both Wagner and Nietzsche, who rejected established concepts of Christian morality. Nietzsche proclaimed that 'God is dead', postulating the ideal of the Übermensch, or 'superman', who would impose his self-created will on the weak and the worthless – a view fully in keeping with the gargantuan nature of the Romantic ego, with its roots in the controlling powers of the Industrial Revolution and the spate of scientific discoveries which granted man an ever greater mastery of his environment.

Nietzsche proclaimed the ideal of the 'superman' who would impose his will on the weak—a view fully in keeping with the gargantuan nature of the Romantic ego.

Kierkegaard, the founder of 'existential' philosophy, was fundamentally out of step with these ideas, taking what was in many ways a specifically Christian stance and arguing that no amount of rational thought could explain the uniqueness of individual experience or account for the existence of God, which could be understood only through a 'leap of faith'. However, his suggestion that exceptional individuals (in addition to God) stood outside the laws of morality did not endear him to the Church.

The man who did more than anyone else to weaken the basic tenets not only of Christianity but of all 'creationist' religions was neither a philosopher nor a theologian but a scientist. The theories of evolution, first set out in 1859 by Charles Darwin (1809–1882) in *On the Origin of Species,* have never lost their explosive power.

Less revolutionary, but still explosive, were the ideas of Sigmund Freud (1856–1939), widely known as 'the father of psychoanalysis'. Although his greatest influence and fame belong to the twentieth century, the essence of his approach was defined in the nineteenth, when he first developed his theories of the unconscious and infantile sexuality. His basically anti-religious stance, treated in his book *The Future of an Illusion,* was distinctly a product of nineteenth-century trends.

The third most far-reaching idea of non-philosophical nineteenth-century thought (non-philosophical in a strictly academic sense) arose from an increasingly widespread concern with natural justice. The Quakers were the first European community to espouse formally the notion of sexual equality, but it was such pioneering individuals as Emmeline Pankhurst (1858–1928) and Susan B. Anthony (1820–1906) who, following in the footsteps of Mary Wollstonecraft (1759–1797), really put the issue of women's rights on the political agenda.

The Arts

In the realm of literature it was the century of the novel, when such writers as Charles Dickens, Émile Zola, Victor Hugo, Leo Tolstoy and Fyodor Dostoyevsky managed both to absorb and entertain, and to lay bare the realities of life for the mass of society who suffered rather than benefited from the effects of the Industrial Revolution. Others, like William Makepeace Thackeray, Jane Austen, Stendhal, George Eliot and Gustave Flaubert, dealt in various ways with the lives, fantasies and pretensions of the aspiring middle classes. Timeless issues of love, death, disappointment and adventure were memorably explored by Sir Walter Scott, the fantastical E.T.A. Hoffmann, the three Brontë sisters, Joseph Conrad, Mark Twain, Thomas Hardy and Robert Louis Stevenson.

It was the century of the novel. It was also the century of the great Romantic poets.

Hoffmann and Conrad, along with Anton Chekhov, Hans Christian Andersen and Guy de Maupassant, proved themselves masters of the short story, and Wilkie Collins introduced a new genre, the detective novel. Meanwhile, dramatists such as Henrik Ibsen, August Strindberg, Chekhov and George Bernard Shaw brought a new realism to the theatre.

It was also the century of the great Romantic poets: Johann Wolfgang von Goethe, William Wordsworth, Heinrich Heine, Lord Byron, John Keats, Percy Bysshe Shelley, Samuel Taylor Coleridge and Alexander Pushkin. Of these, Goethe, Byron, Heine and Pushkin had the greatest impact on composers, prominent among whom were Schubert, Schumann, Liszt, Berlioz and Tchaikovsky. Later poets of importance include Charles Baudelaire, Paul Verlaine, Alfred Tennyson and Gerard Manley Hopkins.

In the world of painting, the greatest figures in the earlier part of the century included Francisco de Goya, John Constable (the most famous of a new wave of landscape painters), Jean Auguste Dominique Ingres (a natural Classicist born into a century of Romanticism, with much in common with Chopin, though not friendship), the arch-Romantics Théodore Géricault and Eugène Delacroix (whose obsession with the distant past arose from a characteristically Romantic distaste for the present), and J.M.W. Turner, who was staggeringly original. Turner's work foreshadowed the development in the latter half of the century of the French Impressionists – Claude Monet, Edgar Degas, Édouard Manet and Pierre Auguste Renoir – all of whom strove to represent nature, and to capture the changing effects of light and movement, mixing their colours on the canvas rather than on the palette. These painters were succeeded by the so-called post-Impressionists – Paul Cézanne, Vincent van Gogh, Paul Gauguin and Georges Seurat – who subscribed to no particular school or technique but sought a more objective, less spontaneous and evanescent style than the Impressionists.

Among sculptors, Auguste Rodin stood in a class of his own– a romantic, a realist and a master of his craft with few rivals. The largest sculpture in the world, however, was the Statue of Liberty, presented by France to the United States in 1884.

At the end of the century came a new family of styles known as Art Nouveau, of which Aubrey Beardsley, Henri de Toulouse-Lautrec and Gustav Klimt were prominent though very different exponents. Equally influential in the realm of architecture, Art Nouveau largely rejected traditional western notions of symmetry, drawing much of its inspiration from the prints and buildings of Japan. It reflected a widespread hunger among western artists for a fundamental regeneration of the

A new family of styles known as Art Nouveau reflected a widespread hunger among western artists for a fundamental regeneration of the creative impulse.

creative impulse, and ranged from the highly decorative to the boldly simple.

In the realm of dance, ballet underwent some important transformations, including the introduction of tights, calf-length white dresses and toe-shoes. The technique of female dancers was developed at the expense of the male, who was reduced to a largely supporting role. In the modern repertoire, the most typical examples of Romantic ballet at its best are *La Sylphide* (1832) and *Giselle* (1841).

Architecture

Nineteenth-century architecture in Europe and America reflected both the Romantic obsession with the past and the new industrialists' concerns with practicality and economy. For most of the century, public buildings tended towards an ever more massive grandiosity, drawing on a wide variety of styles that ranged from the distant to the recent past, often within a single building. A famous example, from 1835, is the neo-Gothic Houses of Parliament in London.

Housing for the working class bore many of the hallmarks of present-day factory farming, consisting in the main of terraced brick houses – small, crowded, lacking in facilities which today we take for granted, and of a soul-numbing sameness. However, with the advent of steel, property developers discovered that a high density of housing, office and work space could be achieved by building upwards instead of outwards, thereby economising on land and cost to themselves. Thus the skyscraper began its dominance of the urban landscape. The most famous of all, the Eiffel Tower in Paris (built for the great Paris Exhibition of 1889), had no practical function whatever, beyond

The skyscraper began its dominance of the urban landscape. The most famous of all, the Eiffel Tower, had no practical function whatever.

being a tourist attraction and a demonstration of modern building technology.

Music

Never has an art known greater changes in so relatively short a time than music in the nineteenth century. When the century began, Beethoven was only twenty-nine, and Schubert only two. Haydn, at sixty-seven, was still at the height of his powers. When it ended, Debussy's revolutionary *Prélude à l'après-midi d'un faune*, often cited, even today, as 'the beginning of modern music', was already seven years old, and Schoenberg (25), Ives (also 25), Bartók (18) and Stravinsky (17) were all fully active. The years in between saw the end of the Classical era and the dawning of Romanticism in the maturest works of Beethoven and Schubert (whose symphonies, sonatas and chamber music reached previously undreamt-of proportions, expanding Classical forms to their outermost limits).

Harmony underwent unprecedented transformations, including the progressive dissolution of traditional tonality by Liszt, Wagner, Debussy, Mahler and Ives. The piano attained its full maturity and became the world's most popular and commercially successful instrument, and the art of orchestration became a major issue, thanks to the pioneering work of Berlioz, Liszt and Wagner. Nationalism became a driving force, especially in Russia (Glinka, Mussorgsky, Borodin, Balakirev), Bohemia (Dvořák, Smetana), Spain (Albéniz, Granados), Scandinavia (Grieg, Nielsen), Finland (Sibelius), Poland (Chopin), Hungary (Liszt), Italy (Verdi) and the United States (Gottschalk, Ives).

The piano became the world's most popular and commercially successful instrument.

There was a major shift from the relative 'objectivity' of the Classical era to the intensely emotional and formally self-generating outpourings of the Romantics. Illustrative, 'programme' music achieved a popularity never approached before or since, and the cult of virtuosity became a dominant feature, thanks largely to Paganini and Liszt. The specialist (i.e. non-composing) performer became the rule rather than the exception (such figures were scarcely to be found in the previous century), and music schools and conservatoires became commonplace. Despite this, the discipline of counterpoint, hitherto among the most highly prized of musical attributes, fell into widespread disuse, though it plays an important part in the music of Liszt, Wagner, Brahms and Richard Strauss.

In the works of Schubert, Joseph Lanner, Weber and Johann Strauss Sr. and Jr., the waltz became the most popular form of the century, closely followed by the Victorian after-dinner ballad. Forms in general polarised, from the millions of piano 'miniatures' and 'character pieces', to the gargantuan music dramas of Wagner, the sprawling symphonies of Bruckner and Mahler, and the extravagantly coloured symphonic works of Richard Strauss. Quite apart from Wagner, it was the century of Grand Opera. Such works were long (five acts) and spectacularly staged (complete with ballet and special effects); the most prominent exponents were Meyerbeer, Auber, Halévy, Massenet, Spontini and Verdi. It was also the century of comic operetta, exemplified by the entertainments of Offenbach, Johann Strauss, and Gilbert and Sullivan. Late in the century came the sometimes grimly realistic verismo school of opera, foreshadowed by Bizet's *Carmen* but most famously manifested in the works of Puccini, Mascagni and Leoncavallo.

It was the century of Grand Opera. It was also the century of comic operetta.

The Russian Cultural Background

It would be exaggerating to say that when Tchaikovsky was born Russian music was in crisis, but it was certainly in the throes of major change. It is rare in musical history that an epoch-making watershed can be traced to a specific date and to a single composer, but the story of Russian music, as we know it, is one of those exceptions. To be very precise, it begins on the evening of 9 December 1836 with the premiere in St Petersburg of Mikhail Glinka's opera *A Life for the Tsar*. The composer himself was a wealthy ex-civil servant (not your normal, fire-in-the-belly revolutionary), but from that day to this he has been popularly known as 'the father of Russian music'. What he did, in that one opera (so goes the folklore), was to provoke a national identity crisis that was to rumble on throughout the rest of the century. This was true, but he did not rest content with a single opera. In works like his second opera, ***Ruslan and Lyudmila***, and the purely orchestral ***Kamarinskaya***, he focused attention on an already existing problem with such force and brilliance that no one after him could afford to ignore it.

Mikhail Glinka has been popularly known as 'the father of Russian music'. Before Glinka, there was really no such thing as Russian music.

It is a strange but fundamentally important fact that before Glinka, as his unofficial title suggests, there was really no such thing as Russian music (except, of course, for folk music – no country lacks that). There was, indeed, music by

Russian composers, but that is hardly the same thing. The fact is that before Glinka such cultural traditions as existed at all in Russia were not only recent but they borrowed almost entirely from elsewhere, most notably from western Europe. While this part of the continent was basking in the glories of Byrd and Palestrina, and later of Schütz and Monteverdi, and later still of Bach and Handel, Russia was still effectively mired in the Middle Ages. In the thirteenth century, when the austerities of Gregorian chant began in the West to give way to the worldly and fascinating miracles of harmony and counterpoint, Russia was to all intents and purposes frozen off from the rest of the world by a social and political cataclysm whose repercussions can still be felt today. She was overrun, and effectively imprisoned for some three centuries by invading hordes of Tartars who belonged originally to the marauding armies of Genghis Khan. Having been, to all appearances, on the brink of a Renaissance akin to the rest of Europe's, Russia was reduced to a smouldering hulk, her wealth destroyed, and all physical evidence of her culture obliterated. Nor, in the fifteenth century, when the princes of Muscovy finally expelled the invaders, did things improve much. The Tartars were replaced by a Tsardom which was partly oriental, partly Byzantine, and which amounted to a system of despotism more repressive than anything ever seen further west. With the imposition of serfdom on the peasantry, the picture of a potentially great nation in a state of semi-barbarous isolation was all but complete.

Russia was overrun by invading hordes of Tartars, reduced to a smouldering hulk, her wealth destroyed, and all physical evidence of her culture obliterated.

There was still another factor, though, which aggravated Russia's increasingly chronic cultural backwardness, and that was the extreme dogmatism of the Orthodox Church. It was not until well into the seventeenth century – the century that saw the birth of Bach, Handel and Scarlatti – that secular music even gained a foothold in Russia. This it did thanks largely to the efforts of one tsar, Alexey, who was the father of Peter the Great. He had the audacity to summon to Moscow a group of foreign musicians whose brief was specifically to instruct the Russians in the playing of western instruments. The reaction of the Church was swift and savage. It issued an order commanding 'that all musical instruments be broken up and burnt, and all mountebanks and jugglers [i.e. musicians] be whipped for plying their godless trade – with rods for the first offence and with a knout for the second'. The knout was a Russian instrument of punishment, the use of which frequently resulted in the death of the victim.

The elders of the Church, though, were fighting a losing battle. When Peter the Great came to the throne he determined to drag his suffering and retarded country into the modern world, by the heels if necessary; and like his father, he did it by looking westwards. In the space of a generation he attempted to import directly the science, industry, art and manners of Europe. To this end he brought into Russia thousands upon thousands of scholars, craftsmen, engineers, musicians and artists. In the century and a half that followed, Peter's reforms were carried on and modified by his successors, and Russian cultural life became ever more indistinguishable from that of Italy, France, or Germany. Musical life in particular was controlled almost entirely by aristocratic amateurs – a tradition that continued virtually unbroken until the emergence, far into the nineteenth century, of Tchaikovsky.

Not only did Glinka's first opera have a Russian plot, it openly glorified Russian folk music and suggested for the first time the possibility of a genuinely national and unmistakably Russian art music.

It was against this background of imported splendour and dilettantism (which took no notice either of the peasants or of the indigenous music that flourished among them) that

Glinka's first opera caused such a sensation. Not only did it have a Russian plot, it openly glorified Russian folk music and suggested for the first time the real possibility of a genuinely national and unmistakably Russian art music. From that point onwards, 'Russianness' became a burning musical issue. But since it had never existed before, where was it to come from, and how was it to be defined and recognised?

Glinka, like all realists, found his solution through compromise. He himself had naturally been trained according to western European traditions, and his music is sometimes a curious blend of Italianate technique with the typical contours, rhythms and harmonies of folk music. Part of his Russianness – the part derived from the peasantry – is deliberately naive, and part of it is extremely sophisticated, revelling in vivid orchestration that veers from the lush, almost purple, to the dazzlingly bright. This feature of musical Russianness is also among the most obvious qualities in the work of virtually all the Russian composers whose music we know today: Balakirev, Borodin, Rimsky-Korsakov, Mussorgsky, Tchaikovsky, Prokofiev, Stravinsky, Rachmaninov, Shostakovich, Kabalevsky and so on. But even by the time Tchaikovsky came to musical maturity, in around 1865, the defining of Russianness had become a very complicated and contentious business.

By the time Tchaikovsky came to musical maturity, the defining of Russianness had become a very complicated and contentious business.

Following Glinka's death, the torch of musical nationalism in Russia passed into the hands of an unlikely bunch of amateur composers, who included an internationally renowned professor of chemistry (Borodin), an army officer and sometime civil servant (Mussorgsky), and a naval officer (Rimsky-Korsakov). But the guiding light of this motley crew was an ex-railway official and protégé of Glinka, Mily Balakirev, whose genius was not matched by anything like his mentor's learning. According to one colleague, Balakirev did not own a single book on harmony, orchestration or theory However, under his determined guidance, the members of the group (which came to be known as the 'Mighty Handful' – though their 'might' was sometimes debatable) learned from each other. They may have lacked Glinka's training but they were, if anything, even more fervently nationalistic.

In describing their operations, Rimsky-Korsakov incidentally highlighted one of the most significant differences between Russian and western European thought:

> *For the most part, a work was criticised by its separate elements; the first four bars were excellent, the next eight weak, the following melody was valueless, but the transition to the next phrase was good – and so on.* A composition was never considered as an aesthetic whole *[author's emphasis]. Accordingly, Balakirev usually introduced new works to the circle fragmentarily; he used to play the end first, then the beginning, and so it went.*

This intense concentration on the experience of the moment is an essential feature of musical Romanticism, but it is also fundamentally Russian. You find the same thing in literature. Progressive, organic thinking, the evolution of ideas through logical development, is not a feature of Russian art in general. But all this posed sometimes severe psychological problems for a composer like Tchaikovsky, who felt his own Russianness very deeply yet revered the western European Classical tradition. In the end, he found the price of nationalism too high, because it was too limiting. All the greatest music is universal and reflects universal experience – and Tchaikovsky, at his best, aspired to nothing less. But the greatest drama of his creative life was his unending quest to reconcile

All the greatest music is universal and reflects universal experience– and Tchaikovsky, at his best, aspired to nothing less.

these two powerful and often conflicting aspects of his musical personality.

Tchaikovsky's popularity is beyond argument, but in the view of many western musicians his lifelong quest was never resolved. For them, he was ultimately too Russian to make a wholly acceptable European, and too Russian to be truly universal. Ironically, his weakness as a quasi-European stems directly from his strengths as a Russian: he feels, by western academic standards, too passionately too often; he expresses his feelings, generally, in the concise and self-contained spirit (though seldom in the style) of folksong; and he displays an almost promiscuous gift for continuous melody. Maybe. But he also perfectly demonstrates what Glinka glimpsed at the beginning: that the true Russian is neither western nor eastern but, uniquely, both at once.

Personalities

Artôt, (Marguerite-Joséphine) Désirée (1835–1907): Belgian operatic mezzo-soprano. Born in Paris, she grew up in Brussels, where her father was a horn professor at the Conservatoire. A pupil of Pauline Viardot-García, she first sang at concerts in Belgium, Holland and England, but joined the Paris Opéra in 1858. She later appeared in Italy, Germany and Russia. In 1869 she married the Spanish baritone Mariano Padilla y Ramos, having earlier been engaged to Tchaikovsky.

Auer, Leopold (1845–1930): Hungarian violinist. A pupil of Joseph Joachim, he lived in Russia for many years, becoming a professor at the St Petersburg Conservatoire in 1868. He taught many eminent violinists, including Mischa Elman, Efrem Zimbalist and Jascha Heifetz. After the Revolution of 1917 he went to the US. He was the original dedicatee of Tchaikovsky's Violin Concerto, which he pronounced 'unplayable'.

Balakirev, Mily Alexeyevich (1837–1910): Russian nationalist composer. Named by Glinka as his 'successor', he was self-taught, but a great inspirer of others. The most important members of his circle were Borodin, Cui,

Mussorgsky and Rimsky-Korsakov. Collectively they were known as the 'Mighty Handful' as well as 'The Five'.

Bessel, Vasily Vasil'yevich (1843–1907): Russian music publisher. He was a fellow student of Tchaikovsky in St Petersburg, where he founded a publishing firm in 1869.

Borodin, Alexander Porfir'yevich (1833–1887): Russian nationalist composer and professor of chemistry. He was much influenced by Balakirev and became one of the 'Mighty Handful'. Among his chief works are the opera *Prince Igor*, three symphonies (one unfinished), two string quartets and a dozen masterly songs.

Bortnyansky, Dmitry Stepanovich (1751–1825): Ukrainian composer. After studying in Italy, he settled in Russia, where his sacred works occupied a prominent place in the Russian Orthodox Church. In 1881 Tchaikovsky was commissioned by the publisher Jürgenson to edit some of his music.

Brodsky, Adolph (1851–1929): Russian violinist. Following his studies in Vienna with Joseph Hellmesberger, he was successively conductor in Kiev, professor at the Leipzig Conservatoire, leader of the Hallé Orchestra in Manchester, and Principal of the Royal Manchester College of Music (now the Royal Northern College of Music). He gave the first performance of Tchaikovsky's Violin Concerto after it was rejected by Leopold Auer.

Bruch, Max (1838–1920): German composer. He was professor of composition in Berlin from 1892 to 1910. His most enduring works are the Violin Concerto No. 1 in G minor and *Kol nidrei* for cello and orchestra.

Bülow, Hans von (1830–1894): German pianist and conductor. His wife, Liszt's daughter Cosima, left him for Wagner. He gave the first performance of Tchaikovsky's Piano Concerto No. 1.

Cui, César (1835–1918): Russian composer, critic and authority on fortifications. He was born in Vilnius of French descent. After studying military engineering in St Petersburg, he became intimate with Balakirev and was numbered among the 'Mighty Handful' chiefly because he supported the group's ideals by his writings. His compositions in the early days were thought of highly by Balakirev, who later revised his opinion of them.

Dargomyzhsky, Alexander (1813–1869): Russian composer. Best known for his final opera, *The Stone Guest* (the orchestration of which was completed after his death by Cui and Rimsky-Korsakov), he bridged the gap between Glinka and the 'Mighty Handful'.

Glinka, Mikhail Ivanovich (1804–1857): Russian composer often called the 'father' of Russian music. His only professional musical studies were with Siegfried Dehn in Berlin in 1833, though as a youth he had impressed John Field and Hummel. Most nineteenth-century Russian composers acknowledged their debt to him, and in the twentieth century Stravinsky (among others) did the same. The most influential facet of his work is the nationalist tendency shown in his two completed operas, *A Life for the Tsar* (1836) and *Ruslan and Lyudmila* (1842).

Hanslick, Eduard (1825–1904): Czech-born German music critic. For many years he was resident in Vienna, where he lectured on music history and music appreciation at the University. He was highly opinionated, and ascribed to Tchaikovsky the discovery of music that 'stinks to the ear'.

Jürgenson, Pyotr Ivanovich (1836–1904): Russian music publisher. He started his publishing house in Moscow in 1861 with the help of Nikolay Rubinstein, whom he assisted in founding the Moscow Conservatoire. Besides publishing Russian editions of standard classics, he issued much music by contemporary Russian composers, including most of Tchaikovsky's works.

Kashkin, Nikolay Dmitriyevich (1839–1920): Russian music critic and professor. He worked at the Moscow Conservatoire from its foundation in 1866 until 1896, and was the author of *Reminiscences of P.I. Tchaikovsky* (1896) plus several more articles about Tchaikovsky, Glinka and other Russian musicians.

Kotek, Yosif (1855–1885): Russian violinist and composer. Originally a pupil of Ferdinand Laub and Tchaikovsky, he became the resident violinist in the household of Nadezhda von Meck, to whom he introduced the music of Tchaikovsky (in which task he was assisted by Nikolay Rubinstein). He gave valuable technical advice to Tchaikovsky during the composition of the Violin Concerto.

Laroche, Herman (1845–1904): Russian music and literary critic. He was a fellow student of Tchaikovsky at the St Petersburg Conservatoire. Later, he became a professor at the Moscow Conservatoire. His literary criticism was written under the pen name L. Nelyubov.

Laub, Ferdinand (1832–1875): Czech violinist. He played chamber music with Liszt in Weimar and taught in Berlin. In 1856 he was appointed chamber music virtuoso to Wilhelm I of Prussia. He became principal violin professor at the Moscow Conservatoire in 1866.

Mussorgsky, Modest Petrovich (1839–1881): Russian nationalist composer. He was a pupil of Balakirev, and one of the 'Mighty Handful'. He was strongly influenced by Dargomyzhsky, and to a certain extent by Meyerbeer. His finest works include the opera *Boris Godunov* (the original score of which is startlingly innovatory and reveals more deeply than any other work the true nature of the Russian national consciousness as displayed in the folk idiom), *Pictures at an Exhibition* for piano, some strikingly original songs, and the orchestral *tour de force Night on the Bare Mountain.* With the possible exception of Borodin, none of the members of Balakirev's circle really understood the importance of these compositions. Tchaikovsky was similarly sceptical.

Ostrovsky, Alexander Nikolayevich (1823–1886): Russian dramatist. He first practised as a lawyer, and later became famous as the author of many historical and sociological dramas. Composers who were inspired by his work include Tchaikovsky, Rimsky-Korsakov, Arensky and Janáček.

Padilla y Ramos, Mariano (1824–1906): Spanish baritone. He studied in Italy and toured Europe extensively. In 1869, he married Désirée Artôt.

Petipa, Marius (1818–1910): French dancer and choreographer. Born in Marseille, he first performed on stage at the age of nine. For his professional debut he partnered Carlotta Grisi at a benefit performance for the actress Rachel (Elisabeth Rachel Félix) at the Comédie Français. After dancing leading roles in Bordeaux and Madrid, he went to St Petersburg in 1847 and became ballet master at the Maryinsky Theatre, where he choreographed numerous classical ballets including those by Minkus and Tchaikovsky.

Rimsky-Korsakov, Nikolay Andreyevich (1844–1908): Russian composer. He began a career in the navy but took to music after meeting Balakirev, whose circle he joined. In 1871 he became professor of composition at the St Petersburg Conservatoire. He was also a prominent member of the 'Mighty Handful'. The transparency of his orchestration derives from Glinka, and his late music was to influence his pupil Stravinsky. He wrote many operas, of which the best known is *The Golden Cockerel*. A number of brilliant orchestral works remain staples of the repertoire, and he also composed some beautiful songs.

Rubinstein, Anton (1829–1894): Russian pianist and composer. He made public appearances from his ninth year, and became one of the greatest pianists of his day. As a composer, though immensely prolific, he is now almost entirely forgotten. He founded the St Petersburg Conservatoire in 1862 and was Tchaikovsky's principal composition teacher.

Rubinstein, Nikolay (1835–1881): Russian pianist and conductor, and brother of Anton. He studied in Berlin. In 1859 he founded the Russian Musical Society in Moscow, and, five years later, the Moscow Conservatoire. He

The Rubinstein brothers, Nikolay (left) and Anton (right)

befriended and championed Tchaikovsky, and though he dismissed the First Piano Concerto as 'unplayable' he later became one of its most famous exponents.

Stasov, Vladimir Vasil'yevich (1824–1906): Russian critic and author. He championed the nationalist school represented by the 'Mighty Handful', a term he himself coined in 1867. He had many ideas (which he passed on to Balakirev, Mussorgsky, Borodin, Rimsky-Korsakov and Tchaikovsky) about opera librettos, descriptive symphonic works, and the use of folk tunes. Balakirev's programme for Tchaikovsky's *Manfred* originated with Stasov, as did the programme for the orchestral fantasy *The Tempest*.

Zaremba, Nikolay Ivanovich (1821–1879): Russian theoretician and teacher. He was professor of theory at the St Petersburg Conservatoire from its foundation in 1862, and taught harmony to Tchaikovsky.

Selected Bibliography

Abraham, Gerald, ed., *The Music of Tchaikovsky*, New York, 1946
Abraham, Gerald, *On Russian Music*, London, 1939
Abraham, Gerald, and **Calvocoressi**, M.D., *Masters of Russian Music*, London, 1936
Brown, David, *Tchaikovsky: A Biographical and Critical Study* (four volumes), 1. *The Early Years (1840–1874)*, 2. *The Crisis Years (1874–1878)*, 3. *The Years of Wandering (1878–1885)*, 4. *The Final Years (1885–1893)*, London, 1976–91
Brown, David, ed., *Tchaikovsky Remembered*, London, 1993
Brown, Malcolm Hamrick, ed., *Russian and Soviet Music: Essays for Boris Schwartz*, Ann Arbor, 1984
Garden, Edward, *Tchaikovsky*, London, 1973
Garden, Edward, and **Gotteri**, Nigel, eds., *To My Best Friend: Correspondence Between Tchaikovsky and Nadezhda von Meck, 1876–1878*, Oxford, 1993
Evans, Edwin, *Tchaikovsky*, London, 1906, 3rd rev. 1966
Holden, Anthony, *Tchaikovsky*, London, 1997
Jackson, Timothy L., *Tchaikovsky Symphony No. 6 (Pathétique)*, Cambridge, 1999
Kearney, Leslie, ed., *Tchaikovsky and his World*, Princeton, 1998
Kendall, Alan, *Tchaikovsky: A Biography*, London, 1988
Lakond, Vladimir, ed. and trans., *The Diaries of Tchaikovsky*, New York, 1945
Mihailovic, Alexander, ed., *Tchaikovsky and his Contemporaries*, Westport, 1999
Mundy, Simon, *Tchaikovsky*, London, 1998
Newmarch, Rosa, *Tchaikovsky: His Life and Works*, London, 1900
Orlova, Alexandra, *Tchaikovsky: A Self-portrait*, Oxford, 1990
Poznansky, Alexander, *Tchaikovsky: The Quest for the Inner Man*, New York, 1991
Poznansky, Alexander, *Tchaikovsky's Last Days*, Oxford, 1996
Poznansky, Alexander, ed., *Tchaikovsky Through Others' Eyes*, Indiana, 1999
Tchaikovsky, Modest, Rosa Newmarch trans., *The Life and Letters of Peter Ilich Tchaikovsky*, London, 1902
Warrack, John, *Tchaikovsky Symphonies and Concertos*, London, 1969
Warrack, John, *Tchaikovsky Ballet Music*, London, 1979
Warrack, John, *Tchaikovsky*, London, 1989
Weinstock, Herbert, *Tchaikovsky*, New York, 1943
Wiley, Roland, *Tchaikovsky's Ballets*, Oxford, 1991
Young, Percy, ed., *Piotr Ilyich Tchaikovsky: Letters to his Family – an Autobiography*, London, 1981

Glossary

Adagio Slow.

Allegro Fast, but not excessively so.

Andante Slowish, at a moderate walking pace.

Aria Solo song (also called 'air'), generally as part of an opera or oratorio. It has a ternary (A–B–A) design in which the third section duplicates (and usually embellishes) the first, and is often called a 'da capo' aria.

Bar (US: Measure) The visual division of metre into regular successive units, marked off on the page by vertical lines.

Bass The lowest part of the musical texture.

Cantabile Song-like, singingly.

Cantata A work in several movements for accompanied voice or voices (from the Latin *cantare*, to sing).

Chorale A generally simple (and usually Protestant) congregational hymn. Almost all Bach's cantatas end with a chorale. Chorales are also frequently used as a basis for instrumental variations (e.g. Brahms's Variations on the 'St Anthony' Chorale).

Chord Any simultaneous combination of three or more notes. Chords are analogous to words, just as the notes of which they consist are analogous to letters.

Chromatic Notes (and the using of notes) which are not contained in the standard 'diatonic' scales that form the basis of most western music. On the piano, the scale of C major uses only white keys; therefore every black key is 'chromatic'.

Coda An extra section, often in the form of a final flourish, that follows the expected close of a movement. Sometimes no more than a few bars in length, it can also be long and elaborate with further thematic development (as in many of Beethoven's works).

Concerto A work usually for solo instrument and orchestra, generally in three movements (fast–slow–fast).

Contrapuntal See 'Counterpoint'.

Counterpoint The interweaving of separate 'horizontal' melodic lines, as opposed to the accompaniment of a top-line ('horizontal') melody by a series of 'vertical' chords.

Development section The middle section in a sonata-form movement, normally characterised by movement through several keys.

Diatonic Using only the scale-steps of the prevailing key notes of the regular scale.

Dotted rhythm A 'jagged' pattern of sharply distinguished longer and shorter notes, the long, accented note being followed by a short, unaccented one, or the other way round. Examples are the openings of the *Marseillaise*, *The Star-Spangled Banner* and, even better, *The Battle Hymn of the Republic*: 'Mine eyes have seen the glory of the coming of the Lord'.

Dynamics The gradations of softness and loudness, and the terms which indicate them (*pianissimo*, *fortissimo* etc.).

Exposition The first section in a piece in sonata form, in which the main themes and their relationships are first presented.

Fantasy, fantasia A free form, often of an improvisatory nature, following the composer's fancy rather than any preordained structures. But there are some Fantasies, like Schubert's *Wanderer Fantasy* and Schumann's Fantasy in C for the piano, which are tightly integrated works incorporating fully fledged sonata forms, scherzos, fugal passages, etc.

Finale A generic term for 'last movement'.

Flat A note lowered by a semitone from its 'natural' position.

Forte, fortissimo Loud, very loud.

Gregorian chant See 'Plainchant'.

Harmony The simultaneous sounding of notes to make a chord. Harmonies (chords) often serve as expressive or atmospheric 'adjectives', describing or giving added meaning to the notes of a melody, which, in turn, might be likened to nouns and verbs.

Interval The distance in pitch between two notes, heard either simultaneously or successively. The sounding of the first two notes of a scale is therefore described as a major or minor 'second', the sounding of the first and third notes a major or minor third, etc.

Key Until the modernism of the twentieth century, all classical music in the western tradition was based on a particular scale (major or minor); this means that a piece or passage based on the C major scale is said to be 'in the key of C major', a piece or passage based on the C minor scale is said to be 'in the key of C minor', and so on. The 'key note' or 'tonic' might be likened to the sun, and the remaining notes to planets in orbit around it.

Major See 'Modes'.

Metre, metrical The grouping together of beats in recurrent units of two, three, four, six, etc. Metre is the pulse of music.

Minor See 'Modes'.

Modes The names given to the particular arrangement of notes within a scale. Every key in western classical music has two versions, the major and the minor mode; the decisive factor is the size of the interval between the key note (the tonic, the foundation on which scales are built) and the third degree of the scale; if it is compounded of two whole tones (as in C–E), the mode is major; if the third tone is made up of one and a half tones (as in C–E flat), the mode is minor. In general, the minor mode is darker, more 'serious', and more obviously dramatic than the major. The church modes prevalent in the Middle Ages comprise various combinations of major and minor and are less dynamically 'directed' in character. These have appeared only rarely in music since the Baroque (c. 1600–1750) and have generally been used by composers to create some kind of archaic effect.

Motif, motive A motif can be seen as a kind of musical acorn from which the rest of a section, movement or entire piece grows. It is a melodic/rhythmic figure too brief to constitute a proper theme, but one on which themes are built; a perfect example is the universally well-known opening of Beethoven's Fifth Symphony.

Natural A note that is neither sharpened nor flattened (see 'Sharp' and 'Flat'). When a 'natural' sign is written in front of a note, it cancels the sharp or flat that would otherwise apply.

Oratorio An extended but unstaged setting of a religious text in narrative/dramatic form, usually for soloists, chorus and orchestra. The most famous example is Handel's *Messiah*.

Ostinato An obsessively repeated rhythm or other musical figure.

Phrase, phrasing A phrase is a smallish group of notes (generally accommodated by the exhalation of a single breath) which form a unit of melody, as in 'God Save our Gracious Queen,' and 'My Country, 'tis of thee.' Phrasing is the apportionment and shaping of music into these units.

Piano, pianissimo Soft, very soft.

Pizzicato Plucked strings.

Plainchant, plainsong A type of unaccompanied singing using one of the church modes and sung in a free rhythm dictated by the natural rhythm of the words. Also known as Gregorian chant.

Prelude Literally, a piece which precedes and introduces another piece (as in the standard 'Prelude and Fugue'). However, the name has been applied (most famously by Bach, Chopin and Debussy) to describe free-standing short pieces, often of a semi-improvisatory nature.

Recapitulation The third and final section of a piece in sonata form. Essentially it is a repeat of the exposition, but it often involves fresh thematic development.

Resolution When a suspension or dissonance comes to rest it is resolved.

Rhythm That aspect of music concerned with duration and accent. Notes may be of many contrasting lengths, and derive much of their character and definition from patterns of accentuation and emphasis determined by the composer.

Scale From the Italian word *scala* ('ladder'). A series of adjacent, 'stepwise' notes (A–B–C–D, etc.), moving up or down. These 'ladders' provide the basic cast of characters from which melodies are made and keys established.

Sharp A note raised by a semitone from its 'natural' position.

Sonata form Also known as 'sonata-allegro' and 'first-movement' form, this was the dominant form throughout the second half of the eighteenth century and the first third of the nineteenth. It is basically a ternary (three-part) design in which the last part is a modified repeat of the first (deriving from the *da capo* aria), but with one very important difference: while the first section is cast in two contrasting keys, the third remains predominantly in the key of the tonic (the key of the movement as a whole).

The three sections of the standard sonata form are called exposition, development and recapitulation. The exposition, which may be prefaced by a slow introduction, is based on the complementary tensions of two 'opposing' keys. Each key group generally has its own themes, but this contrast is of secondary importance (many of Haydn's sonata movements are based on a single theme, which passes through various adventures on its voyages from key to key). In movements in the major mode, the secondary key in works before 1800 is almost invariably the dominant. When the key of the movement is in the minor mode, the secondary key will almost always be the relative major. The exposition always ends in the secondary key, never on the tonic.

In many sonata-form movements, the main themes of the two key groups are of a contrasting character. If the first main theme is blustery or military, the second, in the complementary key, is often more lyrical.

The development is altogether more free and unpredictable. In most cases, true to its name, it takes themes or ideas from the exposition and 'develops' them; or it may ignore the themes of the exposition altogether. What it will have is a notably increased sense of harmonic instability, drifting, or in some cases struggling, through a number of different keys before delivering us back to the tonic for the recapitulation. Since the recapitulation lacks the tonal tensions of the exposition, the themes themselves, now all in the same key, take on a new relationship. In its prescribed resolution of family (tonal) conflicts, sonata form may be seen as the most Utopian of all musical structures

Tempo The speed of the music.

Tonality The phenomenon of 'key' (see 'Key').

Tone colour, timbre That property of sound which distinguishes a horn from a piano, a violin from a xylophone, etc.

Tonic The foundation note, or 'keynote' of a scale or key (see 'Key').

Variation Any decorative or otherwise purposeful alteration of a note, rhythm, timbre, etc.

Vivace, vivacissimo Fast and lively, extremely fast and lively.

Annotations of CD Tracks

Works marked (w) may be heard in full by logging onto the website (see page i).

CD 1

1 Zemfira's Song (between 1855 and 1860)

Full of character, this song takes us just about as far back in Tchaikovsky's career as we can get; his very first 'proper' compositions have not survived. This one may have been written as early as 1855, when he was only fifteen. How a boy could write songs like this at such an age and not cause a considerable stir, even among his teachers and schoolmates, is hard to fathom, but we know that no one was thinking of Tchaikovsky at this age as a future musician. Another boy at the School of Jurisprudence enjoyed far greater local celebrity but never caused a ripple in the wider world. Given the influence that Pushkin was later to have on Tchaikovsky (most notably in *Eugene Onegin* and *The Queen of Spades*), the choice of his verse for this song seems almost prophetic. We hear the gypsy Zemfira scorning her harsh, elderly husband in favour of her lover, who is 'young, brave, fresher than spring, and warmer than a summer's day'. Tchaikovsky treats this song so that it fairly crackles with dramatic characterisation, almost as though it were written for the opera stage.

2 The Storm, Op. 76 (1864) (Conclusion)

Here, dating from 1864, is another remarkably assured piece by a man who, though aged twenty-four, was still a fledgling composer; only one year earlier he had been a civil servant, working at the Ministry of Justice. Although preceded by two small works for small orchestra, this dramatic overture to Alexander Ostrovsky's play of the same name marks Tchaikovsky's debut as a composer for symphony orchestra. Again, despite its considerable originality, fiery temperament and intensity of emotion and imagery, it got the thumbs down from both Anton and Nikolay Rubinstein, and was never published in Tchaikovsky's lifetime. As became his future practice, Tchaikovsky sketched out a preliminary programme for the overture, something he was later to do for *Romeo and Juliet*, *The Tempest* (his second 'literary' storm, this one Shakespeare's), *Francesca da Rimini* (Dante), *Manfred* (Byron), *Hamlet* (Shakespeare again) and *Voyevoda* (Pushkin, out of Mickiewicz). In the event, he departed from the programme somewhat, but it demonstrates that from the start of his career he often needed an extra-musical stimulus to fire his inspiration.

3 Romance in F minor for piano, Op. 5 (1868)

In his lifetime, and long afterwards, this vaguely Chopinesque 'song without words' (it is also vaguely Mendelssohnian) was among the great hits of Tchaikovsky's 'saloniste' piano output. Composed in 1868, it turns suddenly and quite incongruously Russian in its middle section, which makes a surprise reappearance near the very end of the piece – a typically Tchaikovskyan touch. Here Tchaikovsky slips into the rather 'orchestral' style that often makes his piano music, as well as some of the songs, sound as though they are transcriptions rather than original to the medium. Quite untypical of Tchaikovsky, however, is the hint of orientalism that slips in just before the return of the main theme. As befits its title, the piece was written for and dedicated to Désirée Artôt, and it is perhaps not too fanciful to imagine its innocent, almost sentimental, yearning as a reflection of the manner in which he felt in love with her.

4 Romeo and Juliet (fantasy overture) (1870)

Widely regarded as Tchaikovsky's first real masterpiece, this haunting, bewitching, passionate and deeply affecting 'opera without words' (for such in a way it is) was written, rewritten, and rewritten again, in 1869 and 1870, before being further revised a decade later. Unlike many masterpieces, it has never been out of the central orchestral repertoire. Most famous for its unforgettable 'love theme', which has influenced practically every songwriter from Rachmaninov to Gershwin and beyond (particularly in the big restatement by the strings), it might defensibly be described as the greatest work Balakirev never wrote. It was he who suggested the idea to Tchaikovsky, he who provided the original 'programme', and he who badgered Tchaikovsky unmercifully throughout the work's composition. Tchaikovsky supplied the genius (and a great deal more besides) but Balakirev served, if you like, as an inspired and creative editor full of insight. Tchaikovsky at thirty found his own voice in this piece to an extent he had not reached before, and with it he could be said to have become a master, albeit a flawed one. Instead of becoming enraged at Balakirev's effrontery, he showed himself to be astonishingly receptive. There was no lapdog docility about him, but he was ever ready to learn, absorb and develop new ideas. It is in the nature of a genius to be a great learner, and to distinguish between what is genuinely fruitful and what is not. Never was there more delectable proof than here.

5 To Forget so Soon (1870)

Composed at the same time as *Romeo and Juliet,* this is the song, discussed briefly on page 131, in which we find Tchaikovsky, in a sketch, writing the 'accompaniment' before the song proper. Particular attention should therefore be paid to the piano part, and consideration given to the way in which a composer uses the piano in a song to read between the lines so as to provide much more than a mere backdrop to the foreground presented by the poet and the singer. It is in this area that the most gifted songwriters can discover and convey textual meanings of which even the poet may have been unaware. Tchaikovsky had the right idea here, but as so often in his songs he lacked either the particular genius or the will to follow it through. And here is the nub of the frustration felt by many of his great admirers: that he failed to bring to his songs what he had the capacity to bring, settling instead for the conventional, 'well-behaved' and modest resourcefulness of a merely respectable composer. There are the almost inevitable shades of Schumann here, stylistically speaking, but Tchaikovsky lacked his mentor's visionary perception when it came to this medium. The poem is a poignant cry from the heart at the fickle, transient nature of romantic love. The lyrical, 'conversational' exchanges between singer and piano are typical of Tchaikovsky's songwriting (indeed of many composers'), but do they tug at the heart? Is the poignancy of the music a match for the subject matter? The answer must come from the listener.

6 **W String Quartet No. 1 in D major, Op. 11 (1871).** Movement 2: Andante cantabile

In 1871 Tchaikovsky composed what was in effect the first string quartet ever written by a Russian composer (he had actually written an earlier, student work in B flat, but it was never published and only its first movement survives). Little could he have foreseen the phenomenal public success of the D major Quartet. Like *Romeo and Juliet,* it has a luxuriously voluptuous tune, but in this case it is not his own, nor perhaps quite all it seems. It is a folksong that he had noted down in the countryside during a stay with his sister, but unlike the 'love theme' from *Romeo and Juliet* (which is a great melody in its own right), this folksong owes its runaway popularity at least as much to Tchaikovsky's presentation of it as to the tune itself. It is all very simple, and by Tchaikovsky's standards the movement is unusually short (especially for a slow movement). Furthermore, he does very little with it, but what he does do is so right that it goes straight to the heart. Here he manages what he so often signally fails to achieve in his vocal song settings: from a simple tune, he draws out depths and spiritual resonances that illuminate and enhance the expressive essence of a melody, without recourse to any suggestive words. And in this large-scale work (the quartet as a whole, that is) he worked entirely without any sort of programme, 'literary' or otherwise. This was his first extended essay in 'pure', 'absolute' music. In this piece, even more than in the 'impurer' *Romeo and Juliet,* he could be said to have come of age.

7 **W Symphony No. 2 in C minor, Op. 17 'Little Russian' (1872)**
Finale: Moderato assai – Allegro vivo

The so-called 'Little Russian' Symphony is almost excessively Russian, but not little in its dimensions. The adjective of the title refers not to the symphony itself but to Ukraine, which was then widely known as Little Russia (and the nickname was appended not by Tchaikovsky but by the critic Stasov). Though composed after *Romeo and Juliet,* it shows a lesser degree of self-confidence – not by sounding less forthright but by sounding less Tchaikovskyan. Again Balakirev is in the picture – virtually in the centre of it. Much of the work, for all its quality, sounds more like Balakirev than Tchaikovsky, and in this finale, as mentioned on page 156, Tchaikovsky pays homage to Glinka, most particularly to *Kamarinskaya*, that 'acorn' of the Russian symphony. But where Glinka makes his point relatively briefly, Tchaikovsky goes to the opposite extreme – as he was often wont to do, hence César Cui's dismissive observation that 'Tchaikovsky could not be concise. He did not know how to write briefly. Seldom discerning in his choice of musical ideas, he nevertheless let go of them with difficulty.' Even so, when he played this finale to the 'Mighty Handful', they were, according to Tchaikovsky, practically hysterical in their enthusiasm. They were not alone.

8 **The Snow Maiden, Op. 12 (1873).** No. 15: Brusila's Song

Not all Tchaikovsky's orchestral works are 'big'. Not only was Cui harsh (as so often) when he said that Tchaikovsky 'could not be concise', he was also inaccurate. Witness this quirky and very Russian little song from the incidental music to Ostrovsky's fairy-tale play *The Snow Maiden*, composed less than a year after the Second Symphony. Here brevity is indeed the soul of wit.

9 **Piano Concerto No. 1 in B flat minor, Op. 23 (1874).** Finale: Allegro con fuoco

Given that it figures in the repertoire of eighty per cent of concert pianists, and thousands of conservatoire students around the globe, it seems incomprehensible that Nikolay Rubinstein, himself a great pianist, should ever have branded Tchaikovsky's famous warhorse 'unplayable'. Unpianistic it may be, but that's the pianist's problem, not the listener's. If the first movement sometimes sounds as if there are two rival orchestras, starting with the piano's sequence of crashing chords at the opening, that problem has been largely dissipated by the time we get to the finale. The 'Cossack Dance' of the finale harks back to the Second Symphony in being yet another Ukrainian folksong, but Tchaikovsky's development and variation of it are here far more sophisticated than in the finale of the symphony, written two years earlier, and the movement is not only less repetitious but dramatically more concise. If the work is not a 'great' concerto in the sense that Mozart's, Beethoven's, Brahms's or Rachmaninov's are (with the dice loaded so decisively in favour of the bravura soloist), it is the first great Russian virtuoso concerto to occupy a central place in the concert repertoire – and before Rachmaninov's it was the only one to do so. Few would argue that Tchaikovsky's two subsequent piano concertos come anywhere near approaching the same class.

10 **W Symphony No. 4 in F minor, Op. 36 (1877)**

Movement 3: Scherzo (Pizzicato ostinato): Allegro – Meno mosso – Tempo I

By the time he wrote his Fourth Symphony, Tchaikovsky had entered the most critical period of his life – the crisis precipitated by his catastrophic marriage and the events leading up to it – and it shows. In this predominantly dark, turbulent, fate-laden work, he uses his own experience as a basis for addressing universal themes. It is at once one of his most personal and inclusive works, which has struck inner chords of recognition in the experience of countless men and women the world over. Even ignoring the details of the programme he sketched out for Mme von Meck, one might instinctively grasp that the symphony is 'about' fate, the inevitability of suffering, and ways of responding to it. Part of that response is distraction, and, coming after the lyrical but melancholic slow movement, the Scherzo, with its famous plucked strings, could be seen as the first exercise of that prerogative, though even here there is an underlying darkness. For all its textural lightness and brilliant originality this is no Mendelssohnian elfin scherzo out of *A Midsummer Night's Dream*, but its enchantment is just as bewitching.

11 **W Variations on a Rococo Theme for cello and orchestra, Op. 33 (1876)**

(Conclusion)

It is one of the many ironies of Tchaikovsky's life and music that although he loved and revered the music of the mid and late eighteenth century (Mozart's in particular) he struggled all his life with the challenges of sonata form and the structural-emotional integration that was its principal hallmark. Following yet more criticisms of his shortcomings as a symphonist after the Moscow premiere of the Fourth Symphony, he took an eight-year break from his symphonic struggles and concentrated on the less structurally demanding orchestral medium of the suite (another eighteenth-century throwback). But even a year before the Fourth Symphony he had relaxed with another nostalgic suite of a kind, the Variations on a Rococo Theme for cello and orchestra, of which this last variation is one of the most delightful.

12 **Eugene Onegin, Op. 24 (1878)**

Act II, Scene 2: Lensky's aria 'Where, o where have you gone?'

The most overtly tragic moment in the whole opera derives from when the bored, caddish Onegin, at a ball, provokes the jealousy of his friend Lensky by dancing a waltz with Olga, Lensky's beloved. Outraged and insulted, Lensky rashly challenges Onegin to a duel. Onegin accepts, but fails to arrive at the appointed hour. Lensky instructs his second to go in search of him, and in his absence, sensing the worst, sings this aria, in which he laments the passing of his youth and bids Olga an impassioned farewell. His forebodings are justified. Onegin arrives, and in the duel kills Lensky, only to be instantly overcome with remorse.

CD 2

1 **Violin Concerto in D major, Op. 35 (1878).** Finale: Allegro vivacissimo

One of the marvels of Tchaikovsky's creative temperament was his ability to produce some of his best music at times of acute personal crisis. No works demonstrate this more inspiringly than *Eugene Onegin* and the Fourth Symphony. But emerging from crises didn't hurt, as is exhilaratingly evident in his lone Violin Concerto, for which violinists must bless his name daily. This ever-popular work is no more avowedly profound than the First Piano Concerto (that was never Tchaikovsky's intention), but in most respects it sweeps away all the criticisms of the earlier work with magnificent assurance, vitality and inspiration: there is no denying that this really is a well-organised work. The writing for violin is demanding but absolutely idiomatic, the proportions are exemplary, many of the themes are among the best he ever wrote, and there is a genuine integrity to all three movements, both individually and collectively, deriving partly from the fact that the slow movement, which flows directly into the finale (by a masterly stroke that is both backward- and forward-looking), was composed after its two mighty neighbours had already been written. By missing out that transition in this track, we diminish ever so slightly the thrill that the start of the finale produces in its normal context, but nothing can detract from the brilliance and *joie de vivre* of the movement itself, 'introduced' or otherwise. This is the music of a man who has turned resilience into a fine art.

2 **Liturgy of St John Chrysostom, Op. 41 (1878).** No. 11: Epiclesis

Tchaikovsky was not conventionally religious. The Russian Orthodox Church, as such, was not of primary importance to his life (indeed, he had problems with its very orthodoxy), but the traditional music of its liturgies had a formative effect on him, being one of the most significant sources of his essential Russianness as a composer. He wrote relatively little church music, and it comes as no surprise that his best-known and most substantial religious work, the *Liturgy of St John Chrysostom*, was composed when he needed its reassuring certainties most. Far removed from the turbulent emotions of the Fourth Symphony and the intensely personal character of *Eugene Onegin*, it stands as a moving, even austere, retreat from the emotional agonies that he was experiencing at the time – a step, almost literally, into another world.

[3] **Capriccio italien, Op. 45 (1880)** (Conclusion)

Tchaikovsky's self-professed 'misanthropy' was belied by his essential feeling of love for 'the people'. Though his knowledge of true folk music outside Russia was sparse, he particularly loved the popular music of Italy, with its close, almost incestuous, relationship with opera. His overt tribute to this treasury of popular culture, the *Capriccio italien*, of which this is the closing section (and for which he rightly saw a rosy future) is one of his most popular and most instantly enjoyable works, and finds him relaxing, both from the strains of his private life and from the rigours of symphonic thought.

[4] **1812 (festival overture), Op. 49 (1880)** (Conclusion)

As this track makes abundantly clear, Tchaikovsky's musical relaxation in 1880 was hardly confined to the *Capriccio italien*. With the exception of *The Nutcracker* suite, the *1812* festival overture is his all-time biggest hit. Its entertainment values are shamelessly extravagant, its pictorialism literally explosive, and its tunes, including a few unapologetic borrowings (the *Marseillaise* for instance) are unforgettable almost to a fault. The overture depicts the retreat of Napoleon's army from Moscow under the superior might and skill of the Russian military. We join the fray roughly a third of the way in.

[5] W **Serenade in C major for strings, Op. 48 (1880).** Movement 2: Valse

Of Tchaikovsky's three orchestral 'relaxations' of 1880, this is the one that pleased him most – as well it might. Alone among the three, it was written 'from inner compulsion' and is one of his most perfectly achieved masterpieces. Unlike the later *Souvenir de Florence* (also for strings) this was never envisaged as a chamber work. Indeed, Tchaikovsky advised 'the more strings the better'. Like so many of his works, it prominently features a waltz. (Tchaikovsky was one of the great waltz composers, and his waltzes are utterly his own; they are quite unlike those of the Strauss dynasty, but are closely related to the French *valse*, particularly as found in the music of Delibes, whom he admired enormously.) And like Chopin, he often incorporated waltzes into his most serious, even tragic works – the 5/4 waltz in the Sixth Symphony is a famous example.

6 **Ⓦ Piano Trio in A minor, Op. 50 (1882)**
Movement 2: Tema con variazioni (Excerpts)

The trio as a whole has already been discussed (see page 105), and these excerpts from the second movement have been chosen to bear out several of the points made there. Naturally, no excerpt could convey the sheer length of the work. The first movement alone lasts around eighteen minutes (as long as whole trios by Haydn and Mozart), the second for over twenty and the last for roughly twelve. The natural candidate for excerpting was the middle movement, a theme and variations. We hear here the theme and first two variations, followed by a three-minute fugue – as untypical a Tchaikovskyan exercise as one encounters in the major works.

7 **Ⓦ Manfred, Op. 58 (1885).** Movement 2: Vivace con spirito

Manfred, though not formally included among the numbered symphonies, represents Tchaikovsky's return to the challenge of the symphony after an eight-year break. It cost him dear in terms of effort and rewarded him with what he considered his best work to date. However, the cost to Tchaikovsky is the last thing one would think of in connection with this movement: a quicksilver scherzo closer to Berlioz than to Mendelssohn, but still unequivocally Tchaikovskyan throughout. Unusually among his symphonies, the more inward, reflective middle section (very redolent of ballet) is not recapitulated later on, even in miniature – but just when we may think he is about to return to the opening section of the movement, he doubles back and develops aspects of this middle section in surprising ways before fulfilling our former expectations.

[8] **Symphony No. 5 in E minor, Op. 64 (1888)**
Movement 2: Andante cantabile, con alcuna licenza

The Fifth has been enshrined in posterity as perhaps the most consistently stirring of all Tchaikovsky's symphonies. It is deeply Russian in its combination of fate-laden gloom and indomitable resilience, leavened by liberal doses of what many critics have perceived (and not only in this symphony) as sentimentality and self-pity – the drunken, self-pitying Russian is, or was, a stock figure of national caricature. The most obvious unifying factor, as in both the Fourth Symphony and *Manfred*, is the cyclical use of a 'fate' motif, which appears in all four movements. In this predominantly lyrical *Andante*, it erupts a little after the halfway point (c. 7'13"). Heard in unnatural isolation, its appearance (and almost equally unexpected disappearance), lacking any audible point of reference, may seem a lot more irrelevant than in its rightful context. But the influence of this theme on the whole work transcends mere quotation, in however many guises. In one way or another– melodic, harmonic, rhythmic, 'atmospheric' – it provides the basis for much of the symphony. This second movement, the most 'operatic' of the four, both in its melodiousness and its rhythmic licence (numerous tempo changes, from the subtle to the obvious, are specified in the score), provides a wonderful example of Tchaikovsky's ability to change the whole character of a theme without changing the melody at all: listen to how the main theme seamlessly becomes a waltz (though not one you could easily dance to).

[9] **The Sleeping Beauty, Op. 66 (1889).** Act I, No. 7: Valse

Though late in date, following the Fifth Symphony by a year, this was only the second of Tchaikovsky's ballets. By this time, however, it was already inevitable that it would have to contain at least one waltz (could Tchaikovsky have chosen a subject that didn't offer the chance?). Expectations in this respect were confirmed and richly rewarded, and even without the 'package' of a concert-hall suite, such as was to be arranged from *The Nutcracker*, this gem of a waltz has found a life of its own outside the ballet.

10 **The Queen of Spades, Op. 68 (1890)**

Act I, Scene 3: Hermann's aria 'Forgive me, heavenly creature'

Tchaikovsky was no stranger to the experience of romantic love; he had, in fact, many lovers, but failed ever to find a stable, lasting relationship (save perhaps that with his servant Alyosha, though that was hopelessly complicated on account of their different social stations). This may be one reason why the expressions of love that he draws from his male characters often have a particularly urgent and tormented intensity, as though the singer knows in his heart that happy-ever-after fulfilment will be denied him. Hermann's declaration of love to Liza in *The Queen of Spades* is a case in point – and there may be added significance in the fact that his love is declared in the context of apology. 'Forgive me, heavenly creature, for disturbing your repose,' he begins.

11 W **The Nutcracker, Op. 71 (1892)**

Act II, No. 14, Variation 2: 'The Dance of the Sugar-Plum Fairy'

This most popular of Tchaikovsky ballet scores, written in the penultimate year of his life, has come in for more than its fair share of abuse by a coterie of diehard eggheads whose intellectual proclivities oblige them to analyse magic, which by definition and purpose transcends analysis. The historical, or supposedly historical, significance of 'The Dance of the Sugar-Plum Fairy' lies in the use of the celesta, but its place in history has nothing to do with that. Its place in history has everything to do with magic: two minutes and ten seconds of it, to be precise.

12 W **Symphony No. 6 in B minor, Op. 74 'Pathétique' (1893)**

Finale: Adagio lamentoso – Andante

Tchaikovsky's last symphony was not only his greatest, as he himself rightly perceived, but his most influential. Its influence extended beyond the work of other composers (particularly Mahler) to affect the biographical treatment of his own life. Especially in conjunction with his mysterious death soon after the work's premiere, and with his own reference to the symphony as 'autobiographical', the despairing finale (the first slow movement ever to conclude a symphony, and still the most profoundly pessimistic) was quickly interpreted as 'prophetic', and was cited, even before the first biography was written, as 'proof' of his intention to commit suicide. Of course these things are of interest, even though they remain speculation well over a century later. Likewise, they can add something to one's experience of the music. But all that ultimately matters is the music itself, which has long since stood the test of time.

Index

A

Adam, Adolphe **56**
Alapayevsk **9**
Albéniz, Isaac **193**
American Civil War **184, 186**
Andersen, Hans Christian **190**
Anthony, Susan B. **189**
Apukhtin, Alexey **15, 23, 131**
Arensky, Anton **205**
Artôt, Désirée **37, 38, 39, 49, 113, 201, 205, 217**
Art Nouveau **191**
Auber, Daniel **38, 194**
Auer, Leopold **82, 201, 202**
Austen, Jane **190**
Austro-Prussian War **184**

B

Bach, Johann Sebastian **20, 131, 196, 197, 210, 213**
Balakirev, Mily **9, 27, 41–43, 51, 77, 85, 130, 153, 155, 193, 198–99, 201–2, 203, 205, 206, 208, 217–18, 219**
Baltimore **140, 144, 151**
Bartók, Béla **193**
Baudelaire, Charles **190**
Beardsley, Aubrey **191**
Beethoven, Ludwig van **20, 21, 22, 24, 48, 82, 153, 177, 193, 212, 220**
Bellini, Vincenzo **6, 52**
Berg, Alban **86, 181**
Berlin **37, 111, 113, 114, 122, 166, 202, 203, 205**
Berlioz, Hector **40–41, 45, 190, 193, 225**
Bertenson, Lev **175**
Bertenson, Vasily **7, 8, 34, 175**
Bessel, Vasily **202**
bipolar disorder **31–32**
Bismarck, Otto von **184**
Bizet, Georges **45, 58, 76**
  Carmen **45, 46, 58, 194**
Bohonager, Maharajah of **166, 168**
Boito, Arrigo **165**
Borodin, Alexander **9, 41, 77, 153, 177, 193, 198, 201–2, 205, 208**
  Prince Igor **202**
Bortnyansky, Dmitry **101, 153, 202**
Brahms, Johannes **20, 22, 50, 76, 82, 111–12, 113, 124, 148, 194, 210, 220**
Brodsky, Adolph **83, 202**
Brontë sisters, the (Anne, Charlotte, Emily) **190**
Browning, Robert **3**
Bruch, Max **165, 202**
  Kol nidrei **202**
  Violin Concerto No. 1 **202**
Bruckner, Anton **194**
Bülow, Hans von **26, 44, 113, 203**
Busoni, Ferruccio **112**
Byrd, William **196**
Byron, Lord **85, 110, 190, 217**

C

Cambridge University **165, 166, 167**
Canova, Antonio **88, 89**
Carnegie, Andrew **148–49**
Cézanne, Paul **191**
Chaliapin, Feodor **vii**
Chekhov, Anton **116, 190**
cholera, outbreaks of **8, 13, 171, 175–76, 185**
Chopin, Fryderyk **22, 24, 157, 191, 193, 213, 225**
Civil Rights Act (**1875**) **185**
Coleridge, Samuel Taylor **190**
Collins, Wilkie **190**
Cologne **122**
Colt, Samuel **186**
Conrad, Joseph **190**
Constable, John **190–91**
Constantine, Grand Duke **116**
Cui, César **41, 52, 104, 120, 126, 127, 128, 132, 153, 201–2, 203, 220**

D

Dante Alighieri **46, 80, 131, 217**

Dargomyzhsky, Alexander **153, 203, 205**
Stone Guest, The **203**
Darwin, Charles **189**
Davïdov, Vladimir Levovich (Bob) **139–40, 165, 166, 174, 176**
Davïdova, Vera (Tchaikovsky's niece) **101, 120**
Debussy, Claude **61, 193, 213**
Degas, Edgar **191**
Dehn, Siegfried **203**
Delacroix, Eugène **191**
Delibes, Léo **81, 225**
Dickens, Charles **110, 116, 190**
Donizetti, Gaetano **6**
Dostoyevsky, Fyodor **8, 190**
Douglas, Lord Alfred **58**
Dresden **122**
Dürbach, Fanny (governess) **7, 8, 9, 36, 163**
Dvorák, Antonín **104, 112, 121, 193**

E

Eliot, George **116, 190**
Elman, Mischa **201**
Engels, Friedrich **184**

F

Field, John **203**
Flaubert, Gustave **190**
Florence **106, 122, 123**
Franco-Prussian War **184**
Freud, Sigmund **179, 180, 189**
Frolovskoye **115**

G

Garden, Edward **82**
Garnett, Constance **vii**
Gatling, Richard **186**
Gauguin, Paul **191**
Geneva **122**
Gerber, Yuli **56**
Géricault, Théodore **191**
Gershwin, George **217**
Gilbert and Sullivan **55, 194**
Iolanthe **55**
Gilels, Emil **26**
Glinka, Mikhail vii, **9, 10, 35, 41, 50, 52, 81, 124, 153, 156, 157, 193, 195–96, 197–99, 200, 201, 203, 204, 206, 220**
Kamarinskaya **156–57, 195, 220**
Life for the Tsar, A **10, 35, 81, 156, 195, 203**
Ruslan and Lyudmila **50, 156, 195, 203**
Goethe, Johann Wolfgang von **117, 124, 172, 190**
Gogol, Nikolay vii
Gottschalk, Louis Moreau **193**
Gounod, Charles **112**
Goya, Francisco de **190**
Granados, Enrique **193**
Gregorian chant **196**
Grieg, Edvard **79, 112, 165, 193**
Grisi, Carlotta **206**

H

Halévy, Jacques **194**
Hamburg **111, 148, 162**
Handel, George Frideric **20, 196, 197, 213**
Hanslick, Eduard **83, 179, 203**
Hardy, Thomas **190**
Haydn, Joseph **153, 193, 214, 225**
Hegel, G.W.F. **188**
Heifetz, Jascha **201**
Heine, Heinrich **190**
Hellmesberger, Joseph **202**
Hlalol Choral Society (Prague) **114**
Hoffmann, E.T.A. **160, 190**
Homer
Iliad, The **116**
Odyssey, The **116**
Homosexuality, Russian attitudes towards **58, 59, 174**
Hopkins, Gerard Manley **190**
Horner, James **181**
Hugo, Victor **190**
Hummel, Johann **203**
Huneker, James **179**

I

Ibsen, Henrik **190**
Ingres, Jean Auguste Dominique **191**
Ives, Charles **193**

J

Jacobi, Nikolay **174**
Janáček, Leoš **205**
Joachim, Joseph **201**
Joseffy, Rafael **148**
Jürgenson, Pyotr (publisher) **122, 202, 204**

K

Kabalevsky, Dmitry **198**
Kamenka **101**
Kashkin, Nikolay **40, 71, 145, 204**
Reminiscences of P.I. Tchaikovsky **204**
Keats, John **190**
Khan, Genghis **196**
Kierkegaard, Søren **188, 189**
Klimenko, Ivan **35**
Klimt, Gustav **191**
Klin **26, 109**
Koch, Robert **185**
Kotek, Yosif **61, 68, 204**
Koussevitzky, Serge **180–81**

L

Lalande, Joseph **185**
Lanner, Joseph **194**
Laroche, Herman (L. Nelyubov) **18, 23, 204**
Laub, Ferdinand **104, 204, 205**
Lazari, Konstantin de **37**
Leipzig **111, 112, 202**
Leoncavallo, Ruggero **194**
Liebig, Justus von **187**
Liszt, Franz **24, 44, 114, 131, 157, 180, 190, 193, 194, 203, 205**
London **111, 122, 166, 185, 187, 192**

M

McCormick, Cyrus **187**
Magritte, René **46–47**
Mahler, Gustav **86, 163, 181, 193, 194, 227**
Manet, Édouard **191**
manic depression **31, 53**
Marseillaise, The **211, 224**
Marx, Karl **184**
Mascagni, Pietro **194**
Massenet, Jules **112, 194**
Maupassant, Guy de **190**
Maykov, Apollon, *New Greek Songs* **131**
Meck, Nadezhda Filaretovna von **33, 61–65, 72–73, 74, 80, 81, 90, 94, 96, 98, 100, 101, 102, 114, 134, 136, 137, 138, 139, 160, 161, 169, 175, 204, 221**
Meck, Yuliya Karlovna von **137**
Mendelssohn, Felix **76, 225**
Menter, Sophie **142**
Merkling, Anna (Tchaikovsky's cousin) **173**
Meyerbeer, Giacomo **51, 194, 205**
Mickiewicz, Adam **217**
'Mighty Handful, The' **41, 42, 43, 77, 91, 120, 153, 154, 199, 202, 203, 205, 206, 208, 220**
Milyukova, Antonina Ivanovna **64–72, 96–98**
Minkus, Léon **56, 206**
Monteverdi, Claudio **196**
Moscow **8, 31, 36, 40, 41, 44, 66, 67, 70, 73, 91, 96, 98, 99, 142, 148, 152, 164, 197, 204, 206, 221, 224**
Moscow Conservatoire **31, 76, 91, 204, 205, 206**
Moscow River **71, 172**
Mozart, Wolfgang Amadeus **19, 22, 23, 47, 48, 76, 77, 90, 94, 114, 129, 153, 220, 221, 225**
Mussorgsky, Modest **9, 41, 54, 77, 153, 157, 177, 193, 198, 201, 205, 208**
Boris Godunov **51, 205**
Night on the Bare Mountain **205**
Pictures at an Exhibition ii, **155, 205**

N

Napoleon Bonaparte **224**
Napoleonic Wars **184, 224**

New York **140, 142–46, 151**
Niagara Falls **140, 144–45, 146, 149–51**
Nicholas I, Tsar **11**
Nielsen, Carl **193**
Nietzsche, Friedrich **188**

O

Ostrovsky, Alexander **21, 50, 76, 79, 205, 216, 220**
Ottoman Empire **184**

P

Pachulski, Wladyslaw **137**
Padilla y Ramos, Mariano **39, 113, 201, 205**
Paganini, Niccolò **194**
Panayeva, Alexandra **93**
Pankhurst, Emmeline **189**
Paris **45, 89, 96, 111, 122, 192**
Paris Opéra **51, 201**
Pasteur, Louis **185**
Peacock, Thomas Love **128**
Peter the Great **41, 197**
Petipa, Marius **205–6**
Philadelphia **140, 144, 151**
Picasso, Pablo **47**
Prague **111, 114, 120, 121**
Prokofiev, Sergey **91, 198**
Prokunin, Vasily **155**
Puccini, Giacomo **86, 181, 194**
Pugni, Cesare **56**
Pushkin, Alexander **52, 54, 91, 148, 190, 216, 217**

R

Rachel (Elizabeth Rachel Félix) **206**
Rachmaninov, Sergey **80, 103, 130, 157, 168, 181, 217, 220, 221**
Rimsky-Korsakov, Nikolay **9, 41, 77, 101, 130, 153, 198, 199, 202, 203, 205, 206, 208**
  Golden Cockerel, The **206**
  Maid of Pskov, The **51**
  Scheherazade **155**
Rodin, Auguste **191**
Romanticism **191, 193, 199**
Rossini, Gioacchino **6**
Rubinstein, Anton **18, 27, 31, 38, 77, 153, 206, 207, 216**
Rubinstein, Nikolay **31, 36, 39, 43, 44, 45, 61, 79, 100, 105, 148, 153, 204, 206–8, 216, 220**
Russian folk music **27, 41, 43, 50, 76, 79, 84, 91, 103, 153–56, 197–98**
Russian music, repetition in **79, 80, 126, 155**
Russian Musical Society **18, 206**
Russian Orthodox Church **157, 196, 202, 223**
Russianness **77, 152–57, 198, 199, 223**
Russo-Turkish War **184**
Rutenberg, Alexander, Colonel **11–12, 13**

S

St Petersburg **8, 9, 31, 41, 72, 142, 161, 164, 165, 175, 177, 195, 202, 203, 206**
  premieres in **120, 121, 140**
St Petersburg Conservatoire **18, 31, 76, 201, 204, 206, 208**
St Petersburg Philharmonic Society **120**
St Petersburg School of Jurisprudence **10, 11, 14, 15, 16, 23, 166, 174, 216**
Saint-Saëns, Camille **44–45, 165**
Sapelnikov, Vasily **142**
Scarlatti, Domenico **197**
Schirmer, Gustav **144**
Schnittke, Alfred **181**
Schoenberg, Arnold **181, 193**
Schopenhauer, Arthur **188**
Schubert, Franz **76, 124, 190, 193, 194, 211**
Schumann, Robert **24–25, 26, 27, 80, 124, 153, 190, 211, 218**
Scott, Sir Walter **190**
Seurat, Georges **191**
Shakespeare, William **48, 79, 217**
Shaw, George Bernard **190**
Shelley, Percy Bysshe **190**
Shore, Howard **181**
Shostakovich, Dmitry **180, 181, 198**
Sibelius, Jean **86, 181, 193**
Smetana, Bedřich **193**
Sofronov, Alyosha (servant/lover) **98–99, 176, 227**
Spontini, Gaspare **194**

Stasov, Vladimir **11, 208, 219**
Stenbok-Fermor, Duke **174**
Stendahl **190**
Stevenson, Robert Louis **190**
Stokowski, Leopold **26**
Strauss, Johann, II **194**
Strauss, Richard **113, 194**
Strauss dynasty **225**
Stravinsky, Igor **86, 91, 170, 181, 193, 198, 203, 206**
Strindberg, August **190**

T

Tchaikovsky, Alexandra (Sasha) (sister) **4, 58, 140**
Tchaikovsky, Alexandra Andreyevna (mother) **3, 5**
Tchaikovsky, Anatoly (Tolya) (brother) **4, 38, 58, 68, 69–70, 72, 93–94, 96, 111, 134**
Tchaikovsky, Il'ya Petrovich (father) **3, 4, 5, 8, 9, 94**
Tchaikovsky, Ippolit (brother) **4, 134**
Tchaikovsky, Modest (brother) **4, 7–8, 13, 15, 17, 30, 39, 45, 49, 58, 59, 60, 80, 99, 101, 113, 116, 122, 134, 139, 168, 170, 171, 172, 175**
Tchaikovsky, Nikolay (brother) **3, 8, 134, 176**
Tchaikovsky, Pyotr Il'yich

LIFE:
adolescent appearance **14–15**
alcohol, indulgence in **12, 59, 99, 152**
alleged suicide attempts **3, 71, 171–73, 174, 175, 228**
Alyosha drafted into army **98–99**
American tour **140–51**
'angelic' temperament at school **13**
annuity settled on, by Mme von Meck **74**
appearance in middle age **144**
Balakirev's influence on **41–42, 51, 77, 130, 199**
Bayreuth, visit to **20**
Beethoven derided by **21–22**
Berlioz's influence on **40**
Bizet's influence on **45–46, 58**
Brahms disparaged by **20**
break with Mme von Meck **134–36**
cause of death **171–75**
compositional development **14, 18–27, 30, 38, 40–48, 49–56, 74, 76–86, 90–93, 103–6, 116–17, 122–23, 124–32, 139, 152–57, 168–71**
as conductor **2, 30, 40, 111, 120, 139, 140, 144, 145, 149, 151, 161–63, 164, 171**
as correspondent **109**
daily routine **109**
dandyism **96**
death and funeral **175–77**
depression **31–34, 61, 90, 118, 152, 175**
deviousness **2**
early formal composition **14, 22**
egotism **35**
emotional intensity **7, 10, 30–31, 37, 47, 86, 98, 152, 216, 227**
enforced separation from mother **10**
engagement to Désirée Artôt **38**
exhibitionism in music **30**
family moves to Alapayevsk **9**
father dies **94**
folksong, attitude to and use of **27, 41, 43, 79, 84, 103–4, 153–55, 197–98**
Glinka's influence on **50, 52, 156–57**
Handel disparaged by **20**
homesickness, tendency to **95, 139, 146, 165, 174**
homosexuality **14, 15, 36, 37, 58, 59, 97, 101, 172, 174, 179**
honorary degree at Cambridge University **165, 167**
hypersensitivity **7, 8, 30, 37**
insincerity of letters **117–18**
letters, boyhood **9, 13**
linguistic abilities **109**
as 'Mad Russian' **32**
Maidanovo **109, 111, 115, 118, 138**
marries Antonina Milyukova **68**
Meck, Nadezhda Filaretovna von
psycho-sexual elements in relationship with **64**
correspondence with **33, 62–65, 72–74, 80–81, 90, 94–96, 98, 100, 101, 102, 114, 134–36, 137–138, 139, 160, 161, 169**

Ministry of Justice **15, 16, 216**
misanthropy **33–34, 143–44, 224**
money, attitude towards **17, 96**
Moscow, move to **31, 66**
Moscow Conservatoire, professor at **31, 76, 206**
mother dies of cholera **13**
musical antipathies **18–21**
nature, love of **115–16, 118–19**
nervous ailments and breakdowns **7–8, 30, 36, 72, 97, 98, 99, 110, 120–21**
sensuality **37**
sentimentality, aversion to **23**
piano, playing of **9, 15, 22–23**
promiscuity **37**
St Petersburg Conservatoire, attendance at **18, 31, 76, 204, 206, 208**
St Petersburg School of Jurisprudence, attendance at **10–11, 14, 15, 16, 23, 174, 216**
Schumann's influence on **24–25, 26, 27, 80, 124**
shyness **15, 31, 32, 34–35, 36, 65, 146**
tobacco, reliance on **12, 17, 59**

MUSIC:
1812, festival overture **84, 181, 224**
Album for Children, Op. **39 24**
Capriccio italien **84, 224**
Characteristic Dances **40**
Dumka, Op. **59 27**
early formal composition **14, 22**
Eighteen Pieces for piano, Op. **72 25**
Eugene Onegin **47, 52–54, 55, 90–93, 120, 121, 162, 216, 222, 223, 224**
Fatum **51**
Fifty Russian Folksongs **(1868–9) 27**
Francesca da Rimini **46, 47, 80, 82, 90, 217**
Hamlet, fantasy overture **117, 119–20, 142, 217**
If Only I Had Known, song **129**
Iolanta **55, 160**
Liturgy of St John Chrysostom, Op. **41 83, 223–24**
Maid of Orleans, The **53**
Mandragora **51**
Mazeppa **53, 54, 101**
'New Greek Song' **131**
'None but the Lonely Heart', song **124**
Nutcracker, The **55, 226, 227**
Nutcracker, The, suite **84, 160, 161, 224, 226**
Oprichnik, The **51**
Pezzo capriccioso for cello and orchestra **83**
Piano Concertos
No. 1 in B flat minor, Op. **23 19, 43, 44, 79, 203, 208, 220–21, 223**
No. 2 in G, Op. **44 83**
No. 3 in E flat, Op. **75 83**
Piano Trio in A minor, Op. **50 19, 100, 105, 225**
Pique Dame (see Sorceress, The)
Queen of Spades, The **54, 55, 122, 123, 127, 140, 141, 164, 216, 227**
Romance in F minor, Op. **5 26, 217**
Romeo and Juliet, fantasy overture **42, 77, 154, 217–18, 219**
Seasons, The, Op. **37b 25**
Serenade for strings **78, 84, 224–25**
Six Pieces, Op. **19 26**
Six Pieces on a Single Theme, Op. **21 27**
Six Romances, Op. **16 131**
Sleeping Beauty, The **55, 122, 170, 226**
Snow Maiden, The **79, 220**
Sonata in C sharp minor, Op. **80 24**
Sonata in G, Op. **37 24**
Sorceress, The **53, 54, 111, 170**
Souvenir de Florence **106, 123, 224–25**
Storm, The **21, 76, 153, 154, 216–17**
String Quartets
No. 1 in D, Op. **11 103–4, 219**
No. 2 in F, Op. **22 104**
No. 3 in E flat minor, Op. **80 104–5**
Suite No. 3 in G, Op. **55 113, 145**
Swan Lake, ballet **25, 55, 56**
Symphonies
No. 1 in G minor, Op. **13 30, 36, 37, 76, 154**
No. 2 in C minor, Op. 17 ('Little Russian') **77, 79, 156, 219–20**
No. 3 in D, Op. **29 80**
No. 4 in F minor, Op. **36 80–82, 83,**

90, 91, 93, 155, 161, 221, 223, 224, 226
Manfred (after Byron), Op. **58 47, 83, 85, 110, 111, 208, 217, 225, 226**
No. 5 in E minor, Op. 64 **85, 116, 117, 119–20, 142, 161**
No. 6 in B minor, Op. 74 ('Pathétique') **85–86, 161, 168–71, 172, 225, 227–28**
Tempest, The **79, 208, 217**
To Forget so Soon, song **131, 218**
Twelve Pieces of Moderate Difficulty, Op. **40 25**
Two Pieces, Op. **10 26**
Undine **51**
Vakula the Smith **51–52**
Variations on a Rococo Theme **46, 47, 80, 90, 221–22**
Violin Concerto in D, Op. **35 82–83, 93, 157, 179, 201, 202, 204, 223**
Voyevoda **43, 50, 51, 154, 160, 161, 217**
Zemfira's Song **14, 43, 216**

Tchaikovsky, Zinaida (half-sister) **4, 8**
Tennyson, Alfred, Lord **190**
Thackeray, William Makepeace **190**
Tintoretto **88**
Titian **88**
Tolstoy, Leo **19, 21, 54, 103, 116, 132, 154, 190**
Toulouse-Lautrec, Henri de **191**
Turgenev, Ivan vii
Turner, J.M.W. **191**
Twain, Mark **190**

U

Undine **51, 116**

V

Van Gogh, Vincent **191**
Venice **88–89**
Verdi, Giuseppe **54, 193, 194**
Verlaine, Paul **190**
Viardot-García, Pauline **201**
Victoria, Queen **184**
'Volga Boat Song' vii, **154, 157**
Votkinsk **3, 5, 6, 9, 163**

W

Wagner, Cosima **203**
Wagner, Richard **20, 40, 54, 180, 182, 188, 193, 194, 203**
Washington DC **140**
Weber, Carl Maria von **194**
Whitman, Walt **147**
Wilhelm I of Prussia **205**
Wolf, Hugo **124**
Wollstonecraft, Mary **189**

Z

Zaremba, Nikolay **208**
Zimbalist, Efrem **201**
Zola, Émile **190**
Zverev, Nikolay **168**